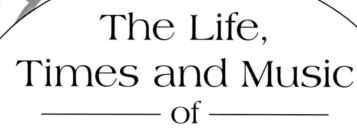

The Life, Times and Music

— of —

Mark Raphael

Gillian Thornhill

authorHOUSE®

AuthorHouse™
1663 Liberty Drive
Bloomington, IN 47403
www.authorhouse.com
Phone: 1-800-839-8640

Published by AuthorHouse   10/29/2012

ISBN: 978-1-4772-3942-1 (sc)
ISBN: 978-1-4772-4260-5 (e)

Dedicated to the memory of
Mark Raphael (1900 – 1988)

Contents

Preface

The subject of this biography is Harris Fürstenfeld, born in 1900, the younger son of Polish Jewish parents who settled in the East End of London. Harris, known as Harry, later changed his name to Mark Raphael and became a well-known lieder singer, a distinguished teacher of singing, a conductor, and a composer of both secular and religious music. This is not a 'rags to riches' tale. It is the story of one who rose from poverty and disadvantage to become successful in achieving musical fulfilment, and recognition in the music world, much of it during turbulent times.

From 1964 to 1968, I was both a pupil of Mark Raphael and a member of his choir at the West London Synagogue. I was one of many whose lives were enriched by his valuable, musical influence. Aware that I was accustomed to putting pen to paper in my job, he asked me to write his biography. At the time, I was intensely busy teaching in the East End and studying at evening classes, so I reluctantly declined. Then I went to America for a few years, and lost touch with him.

Many years later, well after his death, I sadly discovered that no biography had been written, and I was motivated to produce this book, warts and all.

List of Illustrations

The photos of Mark Raphael, family and friends are provided courtesy of Mrs Jane Szilvassy, except those concerning the Taglicht family which are courtesy of Dr Danny Taglicht and Mrs Margaret Taglicht.

Acknowledgements

I should like to thank:

Jane Szilvassy, Mark Raphael's daughter, who gave me unique and detailed information regarding early chapters of the book, and who provided me with family photos; also her daughters, Alexandra Meir and Nadia Szilvassy.

Arnold Raphael, Mark's nephew.

Raymond Raphael, Mark's nephew

Irene Raphael, Mark's daughter-in-law

Dr. Valerie Langfield, whose expert help and advice have been enormously generous and ongoing.

Dr. Michael Jolles who is a mine of information, and never failed to answer my queries despite being hugely busy himself, both as a GP and a writer.

Mark Glanville whose book 'The Goldberg Variations,' his website and personal reminiscences of Mark have been both moving and informative.

Dr. Peter Horton, librarian at the Royal College of Music

Philippa Bernard (Historian of the West London Synagogue)

Geraldine Auerbach MBE

Dr. Danny Taglicht, son of the late Dr Joe Taglicht

Margaret Taglicht, wife of the late Dr Joe Taglicht

Ela Zingerevich, former Director of Music at the West London Synagogue

Sydney Fixman, former Director of Music at the West London Synagogue

Victor Tunkel, Secretary of the Selden Society.

Paul Collen, archivist at the Centre for Performance Studies, Royal College of Music.

Linda Morrell, former librarian at the Royal College of Music

Chazan Michael Isdale

Chazan Dov Speier

Chazan Steve Robins

Michael Leavitt, President of the American Society for Jewish Music

Christopher Bowers-Broadbent, current Director of Music at the West London Synagogue

Sarah Maspero, archivist at Southampton University

Chris Gulley, bass-baritone

Sarah King who proof read this book

Music-Collections at the British Library

The London Metropolitan Archive

The Royal College of Music Library

The Archives of the Royal College of Music

The Royal Academy of Music

The Archive of the V and A at Blythe House, Olympia, London

The Imperial War Museum

The National Archives

The West London Synagogue archives at Southampton University

The archives of Dartington Hall, Exeter

The Centre for Performance Studies at the Royal College of Music

The British Newspaper Archives

The West London Synagogue

The Jewish Chronicle Archives

The American Society for Jewish Music

The Musicians' Benevolent Fund

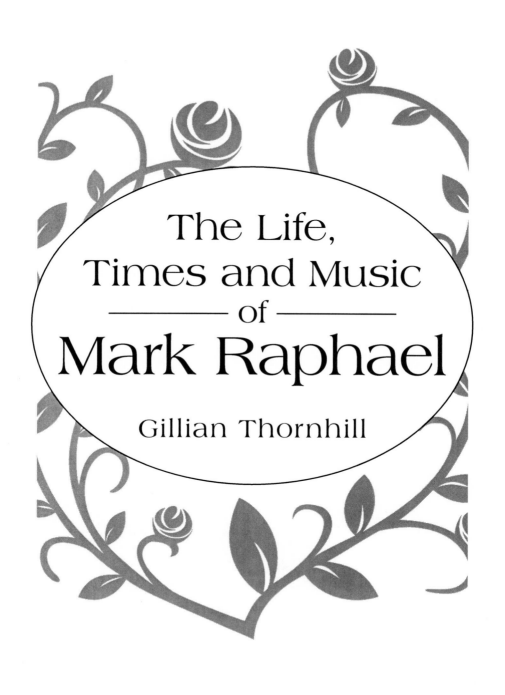

The Life,
Times and Music
— of —
Mark Raphael

Gillian Thornhill

Chapter 1

Origins

During her reign as the powerful Empress of Russia from 1762 until her death in 1796, Catherine the Great extended the borders of Russian territory both westwards and to the south through military conquests and diplomacy. Her initial, liberal intentions towards the Jews were compromised by members of the influential, extreme Orthodox Party who had practised anti-Semitism for many years before. Catherine, herself, perceived no danger to the Orthodox Church from the Jews (rather more from Roman Catholicism, especially the Jesuits), and granted them their religious rights in 1772. 1

Nevertheless, contrary to her original intentions and despite the increase in Russian territory, the Empress was influenced by powerful, political forces to restrict the Jews to a Pale of Settlement in 1791, administered by the Senate and local authorities. In terms of today's geography, it included parts of Lithuania, Belarus, Poland, Moldova, Ukraine and parts of Western Russia. Jews were allowed to live within the 'Pale', or boundary, alongside Christians in these areas, but only a limited number were permitted to live outside the Pale. The intention was to rid Moscow and St Petersburg from Jewish business competition and to remove a so-called 'evil' influence on the Russian masses. 2

Living within the Pale did not liberate the Jews from further discrimination. They were forced to pay double taxes unless they converted to Orthodoxy or served in the military, forbidden to lease land, sell alcohol or benefit from higher education. Even towns and cities like Kiev, Sevastopol and Yalta, situated within the Pale, were barred to them without special residence permits. This situation gave rise to the *'shtetl'*, or small town, within the Pale, where thousands of Jews were crowded together, vulnerable to anti-Semitism. Worse still were the regulations from the Russian government, forcing a large percentage of Jewish young men to serve in the military for a period of up to 25 years! 3

Although during the mid nineteenth century a period of liberalization granted Jews some privileges, the situation was reversed in 1882, following the assassination of Tsar Alexander 11 of which the Jews were falsely accused. As a 'punishment', the May Laws were introduced the following year, disallowing Jews from holding mortgages, buying or disposing of property and from transacting business on Sundays or Christian holy days. They were no longer allowed to move into the countryside, but forced to stay in urban areas within the Pale. Economic stagnation created terrible poverty and hardship, worsened by a series of pogroms to which the government often turned a blind eye. Property was burned, women raped, men beaten up and killed.

The one million or so souls in the Pale in 1800 had increased to over five million by 1897, with the economic structure of Russia failing to expand to their needs; this situation was exacerbated by the anti-Semitism of the Tsarist regime, resulting in a deliberate and heartless oppression. The desire to emigrate became contagious. Between 1870 and 1914 over two million

Jews left the Russian Empire to start a new life in America, Canada, Argentina, Africa, Australia, Palestine and elsewhere. The vast majority chose the United States, often sailing to Hull, on the north-east of England, travelling across the country by train and then transferring to ships at Liverpool, on to their destinations. About one hundred and twenty thousand chose to settle in Britain, the majority in London, others in Manchester, Birmingham, Hull, Newcastle, Glasgow and Leeds. 5

These were Ashkenazi Jews, the descendants of medieval Jewish communities who lived along the Rhine, many of whom had later moved east to non German-speaking areas, taking their language, Yiddish, with them…a Germanic language, yet written in Hebrew letters. In spite of the pograms , and the fact that 5,000 reservists landed in England to avoid military service in Siberia during the Russo-Turkish war of 1877-78, there was "no work, no commerce, the harvest was unpredictable, nothing for the workman to do, and no-one to whom to sell merchandise." The principal reason, then, for emigration was that "they simply could not earn a piece of bread." In Lithuania and the Ukraine, various Jewish international, philanthropic organizations supported as many as 22% of their poor populations. Many of the emigrants were workmen and shopkeepers. 6

The Hebrew and Yiddish press provided reports from England and elsewhere, forming the view in the mind of the reader that England was a free country where immigrants would need to work extremely hard to earn very little, and a fortunate few might become prosperous…like the Rothschilds and the Montefiores.

The principal ports of embarkation for England in the late 19th century were Bremen, Hamburg, Libau (in Latvia, and one of the main ports of the Russian Empire until 1914) and Rotterdam. Dutch Jews had been arriving in England from Rotterdam since the 18th century. As it took time, trouble and money to secure passports, many emigrants did not bother, and those who were conscripted into the Russian army would certainly not try to obtain them. Emigration agents made certain that a number of travellers possessed passports in order to outwit the officials, and smuggled in many with no papers as they travelled by weekly steamer to Hull, Grimsby and London. 7

Many steamships arriving in London docked at St Katharine's Wharf, or at Tilbury. In earlier years, the immigrants were transferred to smaller boats and landed at Iron Gate Stairs near the Tower of London. Usually it was the men who arrived first, and when they had found work and accommodation, the women and children followed.

Those immigrants with relatives or friends already settled in the East End went straight to their homes, whereas others were taken to the Poor Jews' Shelter in Leman Street, Whitechapel, relatively close to the docks. Others, even less fortunate, had to fend for themselves, and often fell prey to conmen.

Newly arrived Jews spoke Yiddish, perhaps Russian or Polish, but no English, knew nothing of London, yet were desperate to earn money. Working for Gentiles was problematic, not only because of the language, but also because Jews refused to work on the Sabbath...from sundown on Friday to sundown on Saturday. This left many with no option but to work for Jewish 'sweaters', usually in the tailoring or boot making trades ,who often exploited the immigrants by forcing them to work for long hours in appalling conditions. 9

A long-established community of prosperous middle-class Sephardic Jews, whose ancestors originated from Spain and Portugal and whose entry into this country dated back to the time of Oliver Cromwell in the 17th century, were living comfortably in the West End alongside wealthy German Jews. Both groups were utterly appalled by the thousands of poverty stricken immigrants who were pouring into London's East End during the latter part of the 19th century. They viewed the incomers with distaste and hostile contempt, encouraging them to move out to the suburbs as soon as possible, or better still, to travel on to Liverpool and to the New World. Many did. The Jewish

Board of Guardians, formed in 1858, paid for the repatriation of 31,000 'undesirables' back to Eastern Europe. 10.

The Jewish Board of Guardians, a well-established, financial elite, were concerned with charitable assistance and basic job training for the poor. The Poor Jews' Temporary Shelter was set up by F.D.Mocatta and others to provide immigrants with a bed for the night after disembarkation, and to assist them with employment. No immigrant was allowed to spend more than 14 nights in the Shelter. A Jewish Bread, Meat and Coal Society and Soup Kitchen provided those items for immigrants in need, and the Jews' Free School provided for the education of their children. Free meals and uniforms were also available for the needy. At one point, there were more than 4,000 pupils on roll. 11

The flow of Jewish Immigration into the East End was stemmed to a large extent in 1905 by the introduction of the Aliens Act. By that time, tens of thousands had made their homes in Whitechapel, Aldgate, Shoreditch, Stepney and Bethnal Green, often living in damp, overcrowded, unhealthy and insanitary housing alongside the native English Cockneys and the immigrant Irish with whom they had nothing in common… except poverty. The English and Irish often moved out of those areas, and more Jews moved in, creating an unintended ghetto.

All was not joy and gladness. Several tensions existed. Christians blamed the immigrant Jews for taking their jobs, for raising the rents, for trading on Sundays and for being different. Jews feared their loss of identity and their Sabbath. Working-class communities were notoriously unwelcoming to outsiders generally so that Jews and Gentiles had little to do with each other. They did not share the same religion, eat the same food, speak the same language, or, for the most part, send their children to the same schools. Fights sometimes broke out, fuelled by alcohol among the Irish and English. Unhealthy housing, combined with similar working conditions, caused substantial numbers to succumb to tuberculosis and other poverty diseases. 12

Having lived in ghettos and among persecution for so long when in Russia, the immigrant Jews had clung to their religion and to each other against the world, studying the Torah and the Talmud and taking strength from their Jewish heritage. They wished to maintain their Polish/Russian traditions and to raise their children in the same way. One way of doing this was to insist that their sons attend a *cheder* in the evenings after regular school where they received instruction in religion and Hebrew. The teaching was mostly in Yiddish, sometimes in English, and the parents often made sacrifices to pay for this religious tuition. The children did not remain at the *cheder* for more than three hours each evening, receiving no instruction on Friday or Saturday, and only two hours on Sunday afternoons. Despite this, at the turn of the century, Lord Rothschild sent a circular to the parents of children at the Jews' Free School, of which he was president, advising them not to endanger their children's health by the excessive hours of the *cheder*. For the most part, his advice was not appreciated. 13

The contempt with which the Anglo-Jews regarded the immigrants was reciprocated in full measure. The foreigners scoffed at their lack of religious observance and their ignorance of the Talmud, refusing to worship with them and referring to England as a godless, commercial country. Instead of attending the Great Synagogue in Duke's Place, Bevis Marks or any of the large London Synagogues, they preferred to belong to *hebrot*, that is to say minor places of worship with a support network, which had been their custom in Russia. They wished to continue their religious life as it had been in the Pale, partly out of familiarity in a foreign land, but also because they objected to the religious manners and customs of English Jews. Additionally, few immigrants could afford to belong to a main synagogue. 14

As Orthodox groups were persuading immigrant Jewry to establish an independent community and English Jews wished to move towards Reform, not to mention an increasing number who no longer observed the Sabbath, Chief Rabbi Adler was concerned about fragmentation and schism and sought the advice of rabbis on the continent. At one point, it was rumoured that the West End Sephardic Community threatened to withdraw their charitable assistance if the immigrants did not acknowledge the authority of the Chief Rabbi.

Just before the death of Chief Rabbi Adler in 1911, immigrant Jewry had somewhat matured. Rabbis from all parts of Britain convened in Leeds to discuss many matters of dissension, ranging from ritual baths and phylacteries to the necessity of Jewish married women to shave their heads and wear a wig, to the dangers of theatres and dance halls. More important was the selection of a new Chief Rabbi, Herman Hertz, Hungarian by birth and American in education, in the hope that his commanding and charismatic presence would provide a unifying influence on Jewry in England.

1. Encyclopaedia Britannica
2. The New Standard Jewish Encyclopaedia
3. Pale of Settlement: Jewish Virtual Library
4. The May Laws: Jewish Virtual Library
5. The Jewish Immigrant in England 'by Lloyd P. Gartner, p.21
6. Lloyd Gartner, p.48
7. The Pale of Settlement. Wikipedia
8. Consul at Riga 1896 F.O. Gartner, p.31
9. 'The Jews of London: From Diaspora to Whitechapel' by Rosemary O'Day (LSE)
10. Lloyd Gartner p.51
11. Jewish reference books at the London Metropolitan Archive
12. 'The Jew in London' by Russell and Lewis , pp. 54 &55
13. Russell and Lewis, p. 216
14. Gartner, p.218

Chapter 2

The East End

Among the many Jewish immigrants who settled in London's East End during the late nineteenth century were Barnet Furstenfeld and Yetta Crook (this surname was given to her, and not originally her own). The family story handed down was that Barnet had been studying medicine at Warsaw University, but had not yet gained his final qualifications, when he fell in love with a young, illiterate glove maker whose parents and sister had decided to emigrate. 1. As Barnet's parents disapproved of the match, and who knows, there may have been other cogent reasons for wanting to curtail his studies…for instance, anticipated conscription into the Tsar's army…he decided to join this mass migration and leave Poland which at that time formed part of the Russian Empire.

The couple were married on 20th June 1897, at the East London Synagogue in the parish of Mile End Old Town. They initially went to live in Cable Street, Stepney, in a truly depressing area known for its prostitution and crime; piles of stinking, uncollected refuse polluted both the streets and the overcrowded houses where Jews, Irish and English lived alongside each other, not always harmoniously. The inconsistent water supply and problems with sewerage worsened the insanitary conditions. Barnet earned his living as a journeyman doctor, ministering illegally to the medical needs of the immigrants in that area which was a breeding ground for infections and disease.

As an unqualified doctor, he would have charged less, and in desperate circumstances payment was delayed or not received at all. He was always worried that his unqualified status would be discovered by the British authorities, resulting in trouble for him in the future, so in consequence, on legal documents, he would protect himself from detection by giving a false employment, for example, cabinet maker or slipper maker. It may well be that out of poverty, he and Yetta flitted or moonlighted to avoid paying rent arrears, a custom not uncommon in the East End, among Jew and Gentile alike. Far more educated than many of his fellow immigrants, Barnet needed to complete his medical degree, but lack of finances prevented him from doing so.

Some time before the birth of their first child, Barnet and Yetta moved into accommodation at 22 Grey Eagle Street, Spitalfields, in a barely improved environment. By settling in tight-knit communities, preferably with those who had come from the same town or village in Poland, the immigrants could retain their own culture and traditions. On 23rd October 1898 their first son, Jacob, was born, known throughout his life as Jack. Less than eighteen months later, the family had moved yet again, this time to 13 Great Pearl Street, not far from their previous address, a bad area of extreme poverty and crime. Here Harris or Harry (the subject of this biography, who was later to change his name to Mark Raphael) was born on 7th April, 1900. In his mature years, Mark always referred to himself jokingly as, 'the same age as the Queen Mother, or as old as the century'.

It can be assumed that with crowds of people living in insanitary conditions, infections and disease were rife, and that Barnet was called out both during the night and day. With lack of sleep and exposed to many infections, his health became undermined, and he caught influenza during the 1900 epidemic. Six weeks after Harry's birth, he tragically died, leaving Yetta with two tiny children to bring up on her own.

As a young widow, unable to work, with very young children dependent on her, Yetta would almost certainly have sought help from the Jewish Board of Guardians, by means of the Soup Kitchens, the Jewish Bread Meat and Coal Society, and relief in cash. Also help may well have come from other immigrants, offering tiny amounts in small synagogue congregations, friendly societies and trade unions. Jewish charity was well-organized and generous to the needy.

Despite the charitable giving, life would have been bleak for Yetta and her two fatherless children. As a small boy, Harry remembered sitting on doorsteps or kerbs staring adenoidally into space, almost always with a cold. As an older child, he remembered standing in queues for the Soup Kitchen along with others in need.

Yetta was too proud to go on accepting charity indefinitely, so she moved to a shop in Hare Street, Brick Lane, where she was able to combine the task of earning her living and looking after Jack and Harry at the same time, selling second hand clothing to her fellow immigrants. At the back of the shop the accommodation comprised two rooms, plus a kitchen, and there she stayed as a widow with her two boys for about seven years. According to Charles Booth's poverty map of 1898, Hare Street was a slight improvement on Cable Street and Great Pearl Street, but only just, and the railway noise in such close proximity would have been a constant problem. 2.

The time came for Jack to be enrolled at Jews' Free School in Bell Lane, Spitalfields, not far from the famous Petticoat Lane, and Harry followed less than two years later. JFS, as it is called, was founded in 1817 and was generously supported from the beginning by wealthy donors, such as the Rothschilds, Goldsmids, Montefiores and the Mocattas. At first only about two dozen boys attended, but due to heavy immigration, by 1900 over 4,000 pupils were on roll, including girls, though in a separate department. It became the biggest school in Europe. In 1902 the cost of State school education, including Jews' Free School, was financed by the State, except for building maintenance and the teaching of religion. Expansion of JFS was mostly due to the ongoing financial support of the Rothschilds. By 1905, when both Jack and Harry had already started school, the Education Act of 1870, creating a national system of elementary education, was well installed. 3.

The educational aims of JFS in the early 1900s were greatly influenced by a former, long-serving headmaster, Moses Angel. A stern disciplinarian who patrolled the school constantly, he was determined to keep the Jewish faith alive among his pupils, but was equally keen for them to adopt English culture and customs. He firmly discouraged the use of Yiddish which he regarded as unintelligible. Like the majority of pupils, Jack and Harry spoke only Yiddish when they started school. According to a Board of Trade report, 'Jewish children, as aliens or born of aliens, enter the school as Russians and Poles, and emerge from it almost indistinguishable from English children'. 4.

Israel Zangwill, the famous novelist of the late 19^t and early 20th centuries, who had been both a pupil and a teacher of JFS remained closely in touch with the school until his death in 1926. His vivid description of the pupils gravitating towards school in the early morning evokes one aspect of life in the ghetto.

'It was the bell of the great Ghetto school, summoning its pupils from the reeking courts and alleys, from the garrets and the cellars, calling them to come and be Anglicised. And they came …a great straggling procession recruited from every lane and by-way; big children and little children; boys in blackening corduroy and girls in washed-out cotton; tidy children and ragged children; children in great shapeless boots gaping at the toes; sickly children and sturdy children and diseased children; bright-eyed children and hollow-eyed children; quaint, sallow, foreign-looking children and fresh-coloured English-looking children; with great pumpkin heads, with oval heads, with pear-shaped heads, with old men's faces, with cherubs' faces, with monkeys' faces; cold and famished children, and warm and well-fed children; children conning their lessons and children romping carelessly; the demure and the anaemic; the boisterous and the blackguardly, the insolent, the idiotic, the vicious and the intelligent, the exemplary, the dull…spawn of all countries…all hastening at the inexorable clang of the big school bell to be ground in the same great, blind, inexorable Governmental machine.' 5.

For fear of losing their identity, and contemptuous of the religious ignorance of English Jews, the immigrants insisted on forming their own *chevrot* or *stiebels*, often named after the area or village from which they had originated. These were local, small, one-roomed synagogues that developed from the friendly societies of Eastern European immigrants to London, providing them with the kind of religious atmosphere that they were accustomed to in Poland. Over 150 *chevrot* had sprung up by 1900. 6.

Just as important in maintaining their culture was the local *cheder* where Jewish children were taught religious education, including Hebrew, after regular school hours, from 5p.m. to 8p.m. according to their age, and on Sunday afternoons. More often than not, the lessons were taught by a *melamed*, or schoolmaster, of questionable ability, in a small, cramped, damp room where the discipline could be harsh and the boys often tired from undernourishment. Sometimes they were expected to translate from Yiddish to Hebrew when their knowledge of both languages was insufficient to do so. For some of the pupils it became a dreaded burden. Harry relived the miserable experience and abuse of the *cheder* in recurrent nightmares until the end of his life.

More expensive and better organized *Talmud Torah* schools, providing sound teaching, were set up by Anglo-Jewry in Bethnal Green, but the immigrants insisted on maintaining the teaching of Judaism, including Hebrew, in the custom of their forefathers in the Pale. They did not trust English Jews, qualified or not, to do the job. Clearly, thrust together, poverty-stricken and discriminated against in the Pale for so many years, they had turned inwards, studying the Talmud and the Torah in great detail, until they became more than ever their religious and emotional raison d'être. 7.

Jack and Harry were still small boys when Yetta decided to remarry. A new husband could hopefully provide financial support, love and companionship, as well as being a stepfather and role model to her children. Much of the strain would be lifted if only she could find the right person. As it was the custom to employ a *shadchen* or professional match maker, a number of eligible suitors found their way to her second hand clothing shop in Hare Street, to be scrutinized by Yetta, and vetted by her boys who were hiding in the back of the shop, yet still able to see what was going on! Afterwards their opinion was sought and given, and finally they gave their consent to her marrying Hyman Wiseblatt, an illiterate Russian Jew who had been in the military. The story goes that when Hyman was insulted by a Russian officer, he punched him on the nose and fled. Much of his journey across the Pale was on foot, and eventually he arrived at a port where he stowed away on a boat bound for England.

Hyman was a tall, powerful man with red hair and a moustache to match, looking not unlike Joseph Stalin, with a strong singing voice and an infectious sense of humour. Yetta was tiny, but resourceful and capable, her stark experience of life having toughened her. In April 1907, she and Hyman were married at the East London Synagogue in the Parish of Mile End Old Town. They settled down together with Jack and Harry at 18 Hare Street where Hyman was very protective of his new family. After a year or so, Kitty was born, followed by the birth of Israel, known as Pip, about eighteen months later. By 1911, Yetta's widowed mother was living with the family which meant that seven people were occupying three rooms, one of which was a kitchen, affording little chance of privacy. Hyman was employed as a presser for a tailoring firm, but whether it was a sweat shop is probable, but not definite.

At that time, the population of Hare Street and Brick Lane was over 95% Jewish, mostly immigrants from Poland." It was like a ghetto, full of synagogues, backroom factories and little grocery stores, reeking of pickled herring, garlic sausage and onion bread, occupied by exotic-looking people all speaking Yiddish." When, in 1898, the poor, unable to afford more space, revolted against landlords racking up their rents, they were supported by Sir Samuel Montagu and the Rothschilds. In consequence, the Four Per Cent Industrial Dwellings were founded, providing homes with affordable rents for Jewish artisans...shoemakers, tailors, carpenters, cabinet makers...in the area. The Rothschilds raised the money from wealthy business men, guaranteeing them a four per cent return on their investment. Most blocks of flats were built by philanthropic companies, but the need for housing was so great that improvements seemed slow. 8.

On Sunday mornings the Club Row Market extended into Hare Street and Brick Lane, with stall holders selling live chickens and all sorts of animals; from puppies to ferrets, white mice to pink eyed rats, goats, hedgehogs, guinea pigs and tortoises. Song birds were sold as a speciality in Hare Street, chaffinches and gold finches, amid much noise and jostling from a shabby-looking, grimy-faced crowd, whose odorous, unwashed garments, combined with the smell of fried fish. As small boys, Jack and Harry would surely have been fascinated by all this excitement before their attendance at *cheder* on Sunday afternoons. 9.

Important in the lives of many Jews in the East End, both adults and children, was the Whitechapel Library. When overcrowding became unbearable, it provided a warm, quiet environment for work, reading and education; a respite, when the alternative was the street. There were also a number of clubs for boys and girls, set up by charitable and philanthropic societies with the aim of keeping youngsters off the mean streets and to providing further education. The Oxford and St. George's Club, set up by Basil Henriques and his wife, Rosa, was one such club. The local synagogue, too, often provided a social and educational outlet, as well as a religious one. The Jewish presence drove the local prostitution businesses out of the area for lack of custom, with a lowering of the infant mortality rate and less ribald, drunken behaviour. 10.

Harry and Jack would also have been aware of Toynbee Hall in Commercial Street, Whitechapel, founded in 1884 by an Anglican clergyman and social reformer, Canon Samuel Barnett, as a settlement house from which social work was provided with the ultimate goal of lessening poverty. The idea of an educational settlement movement came from the Quakers in the north of England. Educational courses were set up at Toynbee Hall, attracting strong, undergraduate support from colleges in both Oxford and Cambridge with the dual purpose of learning about living conditions in a poor area, and providing help where it was needed, to both Jews and Gentiles.

For Harry, music generally, and singing in particular, became a passion quite early on, and he longed for a piano. He may well have sung in productions at Jews' Free School or at the Hare Street Synagogue for a while, but was soon to graduate to the Great Synagogue in Duke's Place, known as the Ashkenazi Cathedral. The choir master there was the distinguished musician, Samuel Alman, whose liturgical composition was prolific. He had been born in Sobolevka, Podolia, in Russia, and had studied music at the Odessa and Kishinev conservatoires.

After completing four years in the Russian army, he witnessed the terrible pogram of Kishinev in 1903 which prompted him to leave for London where he became choirmaster at the Dalston Synagogue in 1905. He continued his studies, firstly at the Guildhall School of Music and then at the Royal College of Music, focusing on the composition of opera. In 1908, he was appointed choirmaster of the Great Synagogue in Duke's Place. Harry's singing instruction at the Great Synagogue was of the highest quality, and he was soon to become Samuel Alman's ablest, young chorister; the alto soloist. Alman would write music especially for certain singers...a Sheva Brachot for Katz, the principal chazan or cantor. This involved seven wedding blessings, recited or sung for a bride and bridegroom at their marriage ceremony. He also wrote an alto solo for young Harry aged eleven years, comprising a 'Hashkiveinu' meaning 'Lay us down to sleep', and forming part of the Sabbath Eve service. Unfortunately, this was vetoed by the Chief Rabbi on the grounds that Harry was too young, and the part was eventually given to the tenor, Dubin, much to Harry's disappointment. 11.

In 1910, aged ten, Harry sang with the great Gershon Sirota in a duet in the Great Assembly Hall on the Mile End Road, and then again at the Olympia Theatre, London, which was a special honour for him. Gershon Sirota, born in Podolia, Russia, in 1874, was a tenor with an incredibly powerful and beautiful voice, often referred to as the Jewish Caruso. He sang as cantor, concert singer and recording celebrity and had previously held appointments as cantor in Odessa, Vilna and Warsaw. After touring the United States several times as a concert singer, he returned to Warsaw in 1935 to become cantor at the Nozyk Synagogue there. He died with his family in the Warsaw ghetto in 1943 when it was burned down by the Nazis. 12.

In 1911, Harry was to be disappointed again by failing the eleven plus examination, preventing him from gaining a grammar school education. The fact that Yiddish was spoken in the home and the cheder, with both his mother and stepfather illiterate in English, would not have helped. As a general rule, Jewish parents were very interested in their children's education, and Yetta was probably no exception , but a restriction on the children of aliens being awarded scholarships gave Harry and Jack no chance at all. This injustice was only rectified in 1928 when the Jewish Board of Deputies successfully petitioned the London County Council on the subject. 13.

The year 1911 was one of great unrest in the East End from the start which Jack and Harry would have known about. On 3rd January, following the robbing of a jeweller's shop in Houndsditch two weeks earlier during which three police officers were killed and two injured, a siege took place which shocked the whole of Britain. The gang responsible for the robbery were Latvian revolutionaries who were trying to raise funds to help their fellow activists in Russia and Latvia. When the police were tipped off that the Latvian anarchists were hiding out in rooms at 100 Sidney Street, right in the heart of Stepney, the residents of that address were evacuated, and the army was called in. A siege of seven hours took place between the anarchists and more than 200 hundred police and a detachment of Scots Guards, ending only when the house caught fire. It was thought that the gunmen had caused the fire themselves, and, not wanting to be taken prisoner, they burned to death. This event was well-known to the Jewish community.

Following the relief that the siege was over and the gunmen dead, a sense of anxiety about the immigrant community in the East End pervaded the country, and many called for tougher rules on immigration. Winston Churchill, the Home Secretary of a Liberal Government at the time, did not see fit to change the laws. 14.

In the same year, the dock workers came out on strike, an event which partly coincided with the successful tailors' strike of 1912. In order to break down the hostility between different communities, Jewish families offered to look after the children of striking dock workers who for the most part were Irish.

By 1912, Samuel Alman had become well-known and influential in the Jewish music world of London.He would later become conductor of the Halevi Choral Society and the London Hazzanim Choir, having been choir leader of three synagogues and a prolific composer of diverse music. By 1912 he had written and produced his first opera, *Melech Ahaz* (King Ahaz) in which 12 year old Harry played a minor role. It was the first Yiddish grand opera, and was a mythical story set in the reign of King Ahaz (c732BCE), based upon Abraham Mapu's Hebrew novel ,'The Guilt of Samaria'. The first performance marked the opening of the Feinman Yiddish People's Theatre in the Commercial Road. The theatre, financed by East Enders with £1 shares, was opened by Sir Francis Montefiore, and was a splendidly

Oriental-style building, decorated in cream, blue and gold, with a backdrop picturing a street in Jerusalem. A Magen David hung over the stage. Other performances followed there and also at 'The People's Palace' in Mile End. Then the company went on tour. The opera was well received by the critics, but not by the Yiddish immigrants, with the result that the theatre was closed down six months later, to open again as a cinema. 15.

Samuel Alman was a calm, patient teacher who could not stand histrionics, whom Harry greatly respected as a musician, mentor, teacher and close friend until Alman's death in 1947.

Celebrating his Barmitzvah at the age of thirteen in the Great Synagogue, Harry would have realised that the occasion marked his entry into manhood, triggering thoughts of what he intended to do with his life. Cabinet making, shoemaking and tailoring were of no interest to him whatsoever. Music was all important, yet the obstacles were great. When he asked his mother for a piano, she suggested that when he left school at 14, he should work at the piano factory in Stoke Newington!

Yetta and Hyman Wiseblatt (Mark Raphael's mother and stepfather)

Mark aged 13, at the time of his Barmitzvah.

Mark in uniform as a soldier (1918)

1. Yetta's illiteracy is not surprising. "Before 1925, most Jewish girls didn't have an education. They only knew how to peel potatoes." This summary of the state of education of Jewish girls in the nineteenth and early twentieth centuries, delivered by a European-born rabbi to a reporter from the New York Times in 2000, is fairly typical of the standard picture of Jewish life in Eastern Europe. Eliyana Adler.

2. Website re Charles Booth

3. 'The Jewish Immigrant in England 1870 – 1914' by Lloyd P. Gartner, p.222

4. Board of Trade Report 1894

5. 'Children of the Ghetto' by Israel Zangwill, chapter 3 (one paragraph)

6. 'The Jews of East London' by Rosemary O'Day (LSE)

7. In this case, 'Talmud Torah' is a name given to an elementary school that places special emphasis on religion.

8. Four per cent houses. Lloyd P. Gartner, p.158

9. 'From Heim to Home' by Nina Weiss

10. Whitechapel Library. Dr Fishman p.87

11. 'Samuel Alman, composer', by Elie Delieb

12. Gershon Serota. Wikipedia

13. 'From Heim to Home' by Nina Weiss

14. 'The Siege of Sidney Street. BBC News Today Programme. Sanchia Berg 3/1/2011

15. L.P.Gartner, p.261

Chapter 3

Moving into the Music World

Music Hall entertainment had been popular throughout Britain, particularly in London, since the 1850s, reaching the zenith of its popularity to a wide public in the First World War. Several music halls had sprung up in the East End, including the Shoreditch Empire, The Royal Cambridge Music Hall in Commercial Street and the Hackney Empire. Artists such as Marie Lloyd and Vesta Tilley were received with rapturous applause by East Enders whenever they trod the boards there.

Vesta Tilley enjoyed enduring popularity both in Britain and the United States for over thirty years, becoming the most famous and well paid music hall male impersonator of her day. From the age of six she felt she could express herself better if dressed as a boy, performing exclusively male roles and sometimes parodying male opera singers. When she and her husband ran a recruitment drive during World War 1, her popularity reached its high point. She played characters like 'Tommy in the Trench' and 'Jack Tar Home from Sea', and sang songs like 'The army of today's all right', and 'Jolly Good Luck to the Girl who loves a Soldier.' During her show, young men were sometimes asked to join the army on stage, so it was small wonder that she became known as 'Britain's best recruiting sergeant.'1.

During one of Vesta Tilley's visits to the East End in 1913, Jack and Harry spotted an advertisement for a competition featuring 'Vesta Tilley and the Clog Dancers', to take place at one of the East End music halls. On the day of the competition, Jack accompanied his younger brother, Harry, to the venue for his audition. By this time, Harry, already experienced in solo singing in public, and whose treble voice (within a year of breaking) would have been at its peak, sang his heart out, displaying qualities of a young actor and showman. Harry won the competition, and the prize was to sing with Vesta Tilley and her clog dancers for one week, presumably with the appropriate remuneration. Amazingly, one of the clog dancers was none other than Charlie Chaplin! Forever after, Harry was able to imitate Chaplin's walk to perfection.

His days at Jews' Free School over, Harry left home at the age of fourteen to pursue a brief career in the Music Hall. He appeared with stars, such as Marie Lloyd, as a member of "Carrie Laurie's Juveniles". His speciality was an imitation of Caruso. 2.

By the time he was 15, Harry had decided to change his name from Harris Fürstenfeld to Mark Raphael. He was aiming to become a concert singer and wanted a more attractive, memorable and perhaps a less Germanic name, especially during the First World War...although his brother, Jack, fought on the Somme under the name of Fürstenfeld in the Machine Gun Regiment. In fact, their names were not changed legally by Deed Poll until 1920.

Mark, (as Harry was now called), by dint of necessity, had to apply to the Jewish Education Society for financial help with private singing lessons, very likely with Samuel Alman, the choir master at the Great Synagogue. After about 18 lessons, his voice began to break and he was advised not to sing for another six months. Meanwhile, in November 1915, he applied to the Music

Committee of the Jewish Education Society for tuition in piano playing and composition. Knowing that he had sung under Samuel Alman's direction in the Choir of the Great Synagogue, they listened to him sing 'Spirito Gentile' from Donizetti's 'La Favorita.' The committee considered that he possessed an extraordinarily good voice, ought to become a singer, and was of the especially high standard which was required of new applicants. Mark also played one of his own compositions. 3.

The following month, when the committee met again, Mr Kalisch, one of the members, had tried to contact Sir Henry Wood to hear Mark sing, whilst Mr Solomon, another member, had visited Mark's home and found it to be very poor indeed. Mark's stepfather, Hyman Wiseblatt, was on piece work as a presser for a tailoring firm. Sometimes he earned £2.10 a week, at other times, nothing at all. Hyman said he was willing to maintain the boy to the best of his ability, but clearly he had to support his wife and four children on a low income. Consequently, the Committee agreed to adopt the case, and Mark entered the Royal Academy of Music in January 1916 to study Piano and Composition. The Music Committee granted him the use of their Broadwood piano. At the Education Aid Society concert on 19th January, Mark sang two songs:' Fifinella 'by Tchaikovsky, and 'The Boat Song' by Villiers Stanford. His brother, Jack, who on leaving school had decided to become an apprentice tailor, was conscripted into the army as soon as he was 18. 4.

In September, 1916, Mark's voice had settled down so that singing became his main study, with piano as a subsidiary subject. Throughout the previous months, he had been living at home and travelling to the Academy on the days of his tuition. During the October committee meeting of the JES, Mr Solomon reported that Mark's home circumstances were most unsatisfactory, and clearly he was not getting enough to eat. The need for sufficient food for a growing teenage boy which could not be supplied adequately at home, as observed by Mr. Solomon, would have forced Mark to queue outside the Soup Kitchen for the Poor in Butler Street when he returned from the

Academy in the evening. The Committee resolved to pay Mark £2 for extra food until the next meeting when they would grant a weekly sum for his maintenance. Mr Solomon also noted that as winter approached, Mark did not own an overcoat which he badly needed. The Committee secretary managed to obtain a second hand one for him from friends. Hardship, deprivation and abuse at the *cheder*, created in his sensitive, artistic nature feelings of humiliation which he could not bear to talk about in later life. Reminiscences of the East End almost always distressed him. The pain went too deep. 5.

It would seem that Mr Kalisch of the Music committee had indeed managed to contact Sir Henry Wood regarding Mark's talent because by February 1917, Raimund von Zur Mühlen, the famous teacher of singing, had already auditioned him and the results were extremely encouraging. He considered Mark's voice to be beautiful and quite ready for training; additionally, he found him to be very musically intelligent, considered that he should be trained for opera, and anticipated that he should have a fine career. Mark, on the one hand, did not feel that he was making rapid progress in singing at the Academy, and at the same time, was very enthusiastic about being taught by the Master. The committee resolved that Mark should continue with his piano lessons including general musical instruction, that he should receive two singing lessons each week with Mr von Zur Mühlen, and that he should stay at the Academy only until the end of the summer term before making a change. 6.

Raimund von zur-Mühlen was born in 1854 into an aristocratic family of Russian nationality in Estonia. He was one of the last personal links with the romantic school of Lied composers: Schubert, Schumann, Brahms and Wolf. He studied in Berlin and Frankfurt with Julius Stockhausen and Clara Schumann, amongst others. He was held in love and admiration by all who heard his tenor voice move the hearts of his listeners by singing with great, atmospheric delicacy and sensitive diction. He was able to communicate this heartfelt expression of the Lied to his students, including Mark. He gave many recitals with Clara

Schumann who advised him to perform in London where in 1883 he gave the first of many concerts there. Shortly before the First World War, he finally emigrated from Germany to England where he purchased two houses, one in London and another in Steyning, Sussex. 7.

By May 1917, Mark had already started lessons with Mühlen who had formed a very good opinion of his abilities. He considered that Mark had a phenomenal voice which was still in its infancy, that he should do well if he gave all his time and attention to his studies, and that no efforts should be spared to improve his appearance and personality if he was to become a singer. Mr Solomon urged the necessity for him to be examined by a doctor known to the committee of the Society, and that he should be provided with extra clothes and pocket money when he was invited, along with several others, to von Zur-Mühlen's home at Steyning , Sussex, to spend the summer there. It would give him a change of air and scene as well as constant opportunities to make music, hear music and profit from the lessons to others. 8.

Letters from Mr. Von zur-Mühlen and one of his students to the Music Committee revealed the great success of Mark's visit to Steyning. He was progressing most favourably and one of the other students was teaching him languages, but once back in London it was necessary for him to find a really suitable home. Mark had also written that he would be unable to go back to his own home on his return to London, as his people no longer had room for him. In the Committee's searches, it seemed quite impossible to find a Jewish home where all the other conditions were also suitable, so with the parents' agreement to the religious question being waived, the General Committee arranged for Mark to live at 22 Pembridge Gardens, Notting Hill Gate. They felt that the stepfather was shirking his responsibilities in the matter, and that he was forcing the boy on the Society, a course which the Committee resented. It was therefore agreed that Hyman should be approached regarding a contribution towards his son's support. 9. In defence of Hyman

Wiseblatt, it could be that the family was living a hand to mouth existence, and that he really could not afford the outlay.

With Mark well settled in Notting Hill Gate, it was arranged for him to attend the Royal College of Music where he enrolled in January 1918, citing Raimund von Zur-Mühlen as his guardian. 10. He was to study piano, organ, harmony and counterpoint at the College, would continue to receive language lessons from private friends and singing lessons with Mr. von Zur-Mühlen. At the second Education Aid Society concert, also in January of 1918, Mark sang Massenet's 'Air d'Hérode' and one of Schubert's songs. Some committee members thought that his musical intelligence was being developed at the expense of his vocal technique, but as he had been receiving lessons with Mr Mühlen for only a short time, the overall judgment was that a change often brings about progress in one aspect and less in another until more time has passed and the voice has adjusted. The duration of all this musical education was unfortunately cut short, for as soon as Mark reached his eighteenth birthday on 7th April, he was called up for military service, presenting himself for medical examination on 15th May. The lessons ceased and the Society's piano was returned to its owner. 11.

1. Vesta Tilley. Wikipedia
2. 'If Music Be The Food of Prayer' by Rabbi Jonathan Magonet; an article marking Mark Raphael's retirement from the West London Synagogue.
3. Jewish Education Aid Society records MS 135 AJ 358 (University of Southampton)
4. Jewish Education Aid Society records
5. Jewish Education Aid Society records
6. JEAS records
7. Raimund von Zur-Mühlen
8. JEAS records
9. JEAS records
10. Royal College of Music records
11. Jewish Education Aid Society Records

Chapter 4

Roger Quilter

In a war that wiped out nearly a whole generation of young men, leaving wives, mothers, fiancées and families suffering loss and bereavement on a massive scale, Jack managed to survive hostilities on the Somme, whilst serving with the Machine Gun Corps, suffering only a kick in the mouth from a mule working alongside soldiers in the trenches. Jack recovered, and went on to serve with the Occupying Forces in Cologne until 1920, when he returned to London to pick up the threads of his work as a tailor.

Mark, too young to join up until May 1918, endured a six month course of training, and was on the point of being shipped out to France in November with his regiment (unknown), when the Armistice was signed at Compiègne, thankfully ending the worst war in history to date. Both brothers had survived, and the joyful relief must have been overwhelming for them and Yetta, although Jack would almost certainly have lost friends and colleagues.

After demobilisation, Mark was able to return to his singing lessons with Raimund von Zur-Mühlen, thanks to the continuing financial support of the Jewish Education Aid Society. His need to reacquaint himself with singing in public once more was satisfied by his becoming involved in a number of charity concerts, including one on 2nd January, 1920, at the West Central Girls' Club in aid of the Spanish and Portuguese Orphanage. By the end of the same month, he had made his debut at the Wigmore Hall. The problem of earning money was a constant concern to him, and although he continued to live away from his parents, his need to help them financially weighed on his mind. Yet his attitude to life was positive. In April 1920, Mark changed his name legally by Deed Poll from Harris Fürstenfeld to Mark Henry Raphael; Jack followed suit, but did not change his first name. 1.

The next important aim for Mark was to prove that he was a concert singer, and to develop his repertoire.

It was not until February of 1923 that Mark found himself in the studio of Wilfrid de Glehn, in Cheyne Walk, Chelsea. Raimund von Zur-Mühlen was well acquainted with the de Glehns who were both artists and very keen on the arts generally. Wilfrid and Raimund both had continental backgrounds in common, and the de Glehns would open their home to artists, musicians and singers on a regular basis. Mark's singing teacher, von Zur-Mühlen clearly introduced Mark Raphael into that social circle as an aspiring singer, which is how he first met the composer Roger Quilter, and became his protégé.

The following June, Quilter attended the Wigmore Hall where Mark was giving a recital. The programme ranged from Bassani and Handel to Schubert, Debussy and Negro spirituals, as well as including two of Quilter's Blake songs, 'Dream Valley' and 'Daybreak'. He was accompanied by a black pianist, Lawrence Brown. After the performance Quilter expressed his appreciation of Mark's singing and particularly the vocal interpretation of his own songs. A few days after the recital, Quilter invited Mark to call to see him at his home in Montagu Street. There on the piano was a song written especially for the young Jewish baritone entitled, 'The Jealous Lover', the first of a set dedicated to him, called Jacobean Lyrics. From that day on, a professional relationship and friendship developed which would last for the rest of Quilter's life. 2

The Jewish Chronicle reported in November of the same year, that, 'a noteworthy vocal recital was given by Mr Mark Raphael at the Wigmore Hall on Tuesday of last week, accompanied by George Reeves. We are under the impression that Mr Raphael was heard some years ago; if so, he has since developed his talents, and has now a good voice with artistic power of expression. His singing of a group of Schubert and Brahms songs was particularly good'. 3. Apart from the Schubert and Brahms, the programme included songs by Pergolesi, Ireland, Scarlatti, Quilter and Fauré, displaying the wide range of both his musical and linguistic ability. The Times reported that 'Mark Raphael has a voice of good quality and power.' The Daily Telegraph thought he was 'a singer of outstanding merit.' Following that praise, Mark decided to give another song recital at the Wigmore Hall a month later, involving a group of folk songs by Brahms and more Quilter songs. By this time, Ibbs and Tillett of Wigmore Street had become his agents.

Roger Quilter (1877-1953) was born into a wealthy family in Hove whose paternal roots were in Suffolk. From the 1880s the family seat was at Bawdsey Manor near Woodbridge. He and his four brothers were all educated at Eton, although Roger did not excel academically, or in sport, and hated his time there. He devoted many hours to music, including composition. 4.

On leaving Eton, he continued his studies in music for four years at the Hoch Conservatory in Frankfurt-am-Main since at that time musical education in Germany was considered to be superior to that available in England. Balfour Gardiner, Percy Grainger, Norman O'Neill and Cyril Scott were contemporaries of Quilter and they became known as the Frankfurt Five. 5. By the end of his course, Quilter had made numerous contacts and friends both in Germany and Austria which would prove helpful to him in the future. On his return to England, his career in music was launched at the age of 23 at the Crystal Palace in 1901, when the baritone, Denham Price, sang Quilter's Four Songs of the Sea, accompanied by the composer himself. 6 .

Quilter was very close to his mother who encouraged his music. He was widely read and possessed the effortless, artistic taste of the born aristocrat, whereas his father and siblings were philistines, musically speaking, and took little interest in his career. His own taste was for 'light' 19th century composers, including Debussy, de Falla, Gershwin, Ravel, Sibelius and Stravinsky, but not Beethoven, or Parry.

Over the years, Quilter produced many songs of fine quality, having gained a sound reputation as a composer by 1911, and numerous singers performed them in concerts and recitals. One in particular, Gervase Elwes (1866-1921), considered to be one of the finest tenors of his generation was greatly loved as a human being as well as a singer. Since his vocal style revealed both sensitivity and artistry, he was for many years the main exponent of Quilter's songs. Tragically, in 1921, he died whilst on tour in the United States, accidentally falling between the track and the train at Boston, Massachusetts. 7.

Victor Beigel, the singing teacher and accompanist of Gervase Elwes, founded a Memorial Fund in his memory which later on became the Musicians' Benevolent Fund. He was greatly mourned, leaving Roger Quilter without a principal singer. As a young and less experienced singer, Mark Raphael gradually filled that role, becoming Quilter's protégé, and throughout the twenties he was accompanied by Quilter in many recitals. 8.

Edward Elgar was the first President of the Musicians' Benevolent Fund, and Victor Beigel its first Chairman. Many leading musicians of the day were trustees, including Roger Quilter. Income was slow but steady in the first few years, but received a huge boost when Myra Hess donated the proceeds of her famous wartime National Gallery concerts. Since then, the Fund has grown to be the largest charity of its kind in the UK, helping many thousands of musicians and their dependents.

When Quilter's father, Sir Cuthbert Quilter, died in 1911, he left bequests of considerable value to various members of his family. Roger was left £25,000, with an extra £10,000 after ten years, and another £25,000 on the death of his mother. 9. Following the death of her husband, Lady Quilter had expected Roger to live with her, either in Suffolk or London, so when he announced that he would be moving into his own home, 7 Montagu Street, with his own servants which he could now afford, she was not amused, and only slightly mollified on learning that his house was just half a mile away from her own residence in South Street.

Most young people yearn for their own independence and freedom, but Roger Quilter particularly so, since he was homosexual at a time when homosexual activity was illegal. Liaisons would have to be conducted with discretion, avoiding risk of blackmail. His involvement with lovers could not be conducted in his mother's house, no matter how close she was to him. It may well be that the stress arising from the enforced secrecy of his homosexuality was the root cause of all his periodic illnesses.

Quilter wished the close professional relationship he had with Mark Raphael, and their meeting of minds on matters musical, would provide fertile ground on which a love affair could develop, but Mark was totally uninterested in any kind of sexual involvement with him. He could accept a father/son relationship, but nothing more. 10. Quilter's constant hopeful persuasion would have been frustrating for him, and embarrassing for Mark. In spite of this, he was generous enough to finance Mark's brief trip to Milan in order to take lessons with Emilio Piccoli, an Italian opera singer, and a distinguished voice teacher, with whom many aspiring singers studied at that time; Tito Schipa was a well-known example.

A self-promotional tour to Frankfurt and Vienna followed during the autumn of 1924. Quilter accompanied Mark for part of the trip. He also paid for the necessary concert clothing for which Mark was exceedingly grateful. 11. In Vienna together, they performed ten of Quilter's songs which were received with great applause, and even more warmly in Frankfurt. Although Mark was considered principally to be a Lieder singer (Schubert, Schumann Brahms and Wolf), based on his longstanding connection with his revered teacher Raimund von Zur Mühlen, he was nevertheless able to familiarise Europe with Roger Quilter as an English Lied composer. 12.

Shortly after Mark's return to England, on 16th December 1924, Quilter accompanied him in a group of his own songs, together with works by Chausson and Brahms, involving the Horn Trio with Aubrey Brain playing the horn, at the Lindsey Hall, Notting Hill Gate in a highly successful concert. 13 Roger Quilter's height at 6'3" and Mark's at 5'3" sometimes caused a ripple of amusement as they walked on to the stage together.

The music of the French composer, Gabriel Fauré was much loved by Roger Quilter and Mark Raphael, among many others, so when he died on 4th November, 1924, a Memorial Concert was held in his honour at the Wigmore Hall on 9th June 1925. Mark, accompanied by Quilter, performed *En Sourdine, Le Voyageur and Nell*. Many distinguished artists took part, including Eugene Goossens, Cedric Sharpe, Henry Wood, Olga Lynn and Albert Sammons. Shortly afterwards Quilter invited Mark to Woodhall in Suffolk to meet his mother, Lady Quilter, who, as a widow, was now living in a house of more manageable size than Bawdsey Manor. She was a great lover of music, and much enjoyed the interest and repartee of young people in her company. 14.

Continuing his studies with von Zur-Mühlen, particularly in Schubert and Schumann at that time, Mark sang Schubert's challenging song cycle 'Die Schöne Müllerin' (The Miller's Beautiful Daughter) at the Wigmore Hall on 23rd January, 1925, with George Reeves accompanying. The following May, he gave a final recital, again at the Wigmore Hall, before departing for the Continent, singing Quilter's song cycle 'To Julia,' together with songs by Schumann, Brahms, Fauré, Wolf-Ferrari and some modern Hebrew songs by Samuel Alman. 15.

During the late spring of 1925, Mark returned to Vienna for another concert tour, this time without Roger Quilter, although it was funded by him. They had arranged that Quilter would meet up with Mark later in Berlin for some concerts, but a combination of many rehearsals of *The Rake*, (Quilter's ballet) together with feeling very unwell, caused Quilter to abandon the idea. Mark remained in Vienna, and had to find his own accompanist. Unfortunately, the pianist's hands were too small to cope with the repertoire, and he noted later to Quilter that the accompaniment was ghastly. Depressingly, when his hosts realised that he planned to sing Schubert for his concert, they were not interested since there were many good singers of Schubert in Vienna; the composer's birthplace. As there was no meeting of minds on the subject, Mark cancelled the concert and planned to learn new songs, realising that the programme needed to be settled in advance. 16.

A pupil of Lizst was able to accompany him at subsequent parties where he sang for the rich and prosperous, including a Jewish banker. His audience loved the Quilter songs, and his Schubert singing, according to his hostess, was not to be forgotten. 17.

Mark's comment to Quilter in a letter dated August 1927, is both touching and telling. "I am happy to know that you can with me look in all things without prejudice. The Jew in me thoroughly appreciates it."

1. Deed Poll documents of 1920,provided by Mr Arnold Raphael
2. Roger Quilter: His Life and Music, by Dr Valerie Langfield , p.68
3. Jewish Chronicle, November 1923
4. Roger Quilter: His Life and Music, by Dr Langfield, p.15
5. Roger Quilter: Dr. Langfield, p.18.
6. Sensibility and English Song, Stephen Banfield, p.127

7. Roger Quilter: His Life and Music, by Dr Langfield, p.62
8. Dr. Langfield, p.63.
9. Dr. Langfield, p.37.
10. Dr Langfield, p.76
11. Letter from Mark Raphael to Roger Quilter, 1924
12. Dr Langfield, p.73
13. Jewish Chronicle, December 1924
14. Dr Langfield, p.76
15. Jewish Chronicle, January 1925
16. Letter of MR to RQ 1925 (spring)
17. Letter of MR to RQ, 1925

Roger Quilter and Mark Raphael with unidentified women

Mark as a young performer

Chapter 5

Eva Taglicht

For the sake of economy, during his second recital tour to Vienna, financed by Roger Quilter, Mark was billeted at a school of horticulture located just outside the city. It was there that he met his future wife, Eva Taglicht. She had come to Vienna with her cousin, Lotka, to enrol in a gardening course, and on the first evening at dinner, they were greatly amused by Mark's valiant attempts to chew and swallow the ghastly food served up to them. After each mouthful, he took great gulps of water to flush down the awful taste, and it is likely that their amusement will have sparked off conversation in Yiddish or German, since Mark spoke no Polish. He became very attracted to Eva, a lovely, dark-eyed Jewess with a delightful personality, and she will have enjoyed his inimitable sense of humour and general joie de vivre. When she heard him sing at one of the recitals in Vienna, she fell in love with his voice, and by that time he was already deeply in love with her. 1

The Taglicht family originated from Lodz in Poland, the third largest city in that country, after Warsaw and Crakow. It was known for its textile industry, the Manchester of Poland, and immigrants came there from all over Europe. Poles, Jews, Germans and Russians were attracted by the vision of possible wealth. Some became prosperous, but many went bankrupt. The Jewish masses were struggling with poverty and starvation in the ghetto, and the Russian authorities were not keen on investing in Lodz. It was not until the 1920s that the first sewage system was built, so that life there for the majority was neither pleasant nor healthy. 2. For all that, the Taglichts were middle class Jews and suffered from no shortage of money. Eva was born on 28th January 1904, to Fabius Taglicht and his wife, Sara (née Mendlesohn) ,the eldest of three daughters. Despite the political unrest in that part of Eastern Europe at that time, they enjoyed a happy childhood, spending summers in the countryside, always in the company of a large, extended family of uncles, aunts and cousins.

The Taglichts were secular Jews, that is to say, they were ethnically and culturally Jewish without necessarily having belief in God or being committed to a religious life style. Many secular Jews celebrate Jewish holidays as historical festivals, uphold moral principles of their forefathers and participate in political action, without practising religious Judaism.

As adults, the young Taglichts lived an active, social life in the vibrant cafés of Lodz. Eva's father, a successful textile manufacturer, was able to educate his three daughters. The younger two pursued artistic careers; Rushzka became a pianist and Anjulka was a dancer. Eva herself was the most academic of the three, and was particularly gifted linguistically. Her father, said of her, "She has the combination of the mind of a man, with the delicacy and beauty of a woman". 3. Eva enrolled at Warsaw University, but decided to leave because of rampant anti-Semitism, although it was not directed at her personally.

When the Ottoman Empire, which had controlled the Middle East since the 16th century, was defeated at the end of the First World War, Palestine, with the consent of the League of Nations, was placed under direct British rule 'until such time as it is able to stand alone'. 4. Gradually, Jewish immigration increased, attracted by Zionism offering a homeland for the Jews, far away from the pogroms of Eastern Europe. Unfortunately, in 1920, riots broke out in and around the Old City of Jerusalem between Arabs and Jews which continued for four days. Savage attacks were perpetrated by Arab rioters on Jewish lives and property, out of fear that the establishment of a Jewish National Home would result in huge increases in Jewish immigration, and, in consequence, the economic and political subjection of the Arabs to the Jews.

Despite the problems in Palestine, the Taglichts and the Luxe family decided to emigrate to Palestine from Poland in the early 1920s, and, together with a number of others, became partners in the establishment of the Lodzia Textile Company in Tel Aviv which still exists to this day. As her family had bought a large plot of land in northern Palestine, it was Eva's job, together with her cousin, Lotka, to gain gardening knowledge so as to develop that land to fruitful purposes. At that time it was little more than a desert.

During the same tour of 1925, Mark left Vienna after several performances, often in private houses, to make his way to Berlin where Roger Quilter had provided him with contacts and venues. Quilter was unable to join Mark there as his accompanist, as previously arranged, since he was much involved in the production of his ballet, *The Rake,* and unsurprisingly, he was suffering from bouts of ill health. He was, however, discerning about where a Jewish singer should perform in Germany and Austria, as anti-Semitism was on the increase even in the 1920s. Munich, for example, was very anti-Jewish even in 1925. 5.

Mark's programme included German Lieder: ' Nacht und Traume' (Night and Dreams), ' Musensohn '(Son of the Muses) and' Ihre Stimme '(Her Voice), by Schubert, were followed by a group of Quilter's songs, as examples of English Lied. They were' A Lover and his Lass', 'Blow, Blow Thou Winter Wind,'' Drink to me Only'and 'The Jolly Miller.' These last were particularly well received. Interestingly, some critics thought him to be a tenor, one describing him as 'a tenor with excellent schooling.' Over all, the recitals were a great success and well attended. 6.

Mark's desire to see Eva and Vienna again overruled his previous decision to return to London, and she met him at the station in a joyful reunion. He was fast running out of money and was forced to wire Quilter to send more funds, the problem being that the accompanist needed paying. The additional time he spent with Eva deepened their relationship; their love was mutual, serious and had a future, yet she promised her father that she would do nothing to disturb his peace of mind. Like many before him, Eva's father advised the couple to wait until Mark could afford to buy a small home. 7.

After one more performance in Vienna, Mark finally returned to London on 15th April via Germany and Ostend, feeling guilty about the extra expense caused to Quilter by his prolonged stay in Vienna. Before leaving, he wrote to Eva's father to reassure him about his serious intentions towards his daughter.

Mark's news about his love for Eva created shock and horror to Roger Quilter for a number of reasons. He still craved a homosexual relationship with Mark, and clearly, married to Eva, that would not be possible; that above all he, and he alone, should be the most important person in Mark's life; that Eva was an unwelcome distraction from Mark's main task of establishing himself as a singer; that artists should not marry, and that artistically, a homosexual relationship would give him a sensitive insight into the art of composition, the latter being an ambition of his protégé. Mark remained totally uninfluenced by Quilter's views, yet still valued his close professional friendship with him, and wrote to him assiduously. 8.

The most natural thing in the world was for Mark to write to his mother and stepfather to tell them of his feelings for Eva, but he was quite mortified that they still could not write back, and instead had to ask Pip, Mark's half brother, to write on their behalf. Yetta, Mark's mother, also asked Pip to send her deep thanks to Roger Quilter for all that he had done for her son. In his turn, Roger advised Mark to make more money by increasing the number of his pupils. Mark agreed, but on his return to London, he went to visit Eva's prosperous distant cousin in Golders Green in the hope of financial assistance. 9.

By July 1925, after the Fauré Memorial Concert in London, Mark was back in Vienna again, having assured Quilter that he would do nothing rash, but for him it was the most seductive of cities, both musically and emotionally. He worked out a programme to please the Viennese, including some old Italian songs (Arie Antiche); 'Vergin tutt'amor' by Francesco Durante. 'Intorno all'idol mio', 'Lascia d'amarti' and 'O cessate di piagarmi', together with some of his Schubert repertoire. Mark needed to spend more time with Eva in order to get to know her better. She had the challenging task of talking her father round to the idea of her marrying a penniless singer whose life would take her far away from her family and friends. On 25th September 1925, having finished her gardening course, Eva returned to her family in Palestine, by which time Mark had already left for London. It was arranged that he would visit them the following December in Tel Aviv. 10.

At the end of 1925, Quilter was working on the Five Jacobean Lyrics which he had dedicated to Mark, and wrote to tell him how they were progressing. As planned, Mark was visiting the Taglicht family in Palestine, and had arranged to meet Quilter at Territet, Montreux with Maude Valerie White, the composer, on 5th January 1926. Mark was forced to change his plans, since on that very day he and Eva got married in the Jewish Community Offices of Tel Aviv. 11. Interestingly, both sets of parents had expected their children to marry non-Jews. 12

To say that Roger Quilter was not amused is an understatement. Mark felt that he had no alternative but to cancel his reunion with Quilter, since by law in Palestine the coming marriage had to be publicised for two weeks, with no bending of the rules. It was therefore necessary for Mark to stay if Eva was to be admitted into Britain. Once married, he would leave to join Quilter and company, and Eva would join him later, entering the country legally as his wife. Throughout his stay, Mark was aware of the unsettled atmosphere in Palestine due to the Arab conflict, nervous all the time that something terrible might happen. Yet in spite of the fear and dirt of Jerusalem, he was drawn to the Holy City and wished to return. 13.

During his stay Mark gave one recital, in an imposing house with a very large music room where the audience was mostly musically cultured Russian Jews. He sang a number of Quilter's songs, the first time ever to be heard in the Holy Land, followed by some of Samuel Alman's Hebrew songs. The applause was deafening. 14.

For his part, Jack Raphael, Mark's older brother, had married in 1924, his wife Rachel originating from Glasgow. By 1927 their first child, Beryl, was born followed by Arnold, Gloria, Raymond and finally Cynthia...five children in seven years! Jack joined a partnership in a clothing company known as Raphael, Lewis and Silver, which was successful for some time until the Depression. 15.

The economic situation in Palestine was not as buoyant as Fabius Taglicht and company had expected when leaving Poland, due to house, land and import taxes...some of which were based on those introduced by the Turks fifty years earlier. There were also restrictions on the amount of money which could be taken out of Poland. Therefore, although Eva's father became convinced of the couple's genuine love for each other, which had set his mind at rest, he assured them that he would be unable to help them out financially, as much as he would have liked. 16.

The couple returned to London to start their married life in a small flat in Ordnance Road, St John's Wood, where life for Eva would be very different indeed. She spoke little English, her background was far removed from Mark's in the East End, and money was tight. What Mark earned from his singing engagements and teaching did not amount to a great deal. Eva missed the company of her family and extended family all around her, as they had been both in Poland and Palestine.

When Mark was involved in his work, she often felt very lonely in impersonal London, wondering how to fit into the British way of life. It was around this time that their artist friend, Jane de Glehn,(wife of Wilfrid de Glehn RA) drew portraits of both Eva and Mark. 17.

Back on the London music scene, Mark prepared for a performance of the demanding Schumann song cycle, 'Dichterliebe', which he gave at the Grotrian Hall on 30th November 1926. 18. The sixteen songs are based on part of Heinrich Heine's 'Lyrisches Intermezzo' and are sung as a complete piece of work, usually by a male voice. Taking its place in German romanticism, Dichterliebe tells the story of a sorrowful knight who sits gloomily in his house all day, but at night is visited by his fairy bride with whom he dances until daylight. He sings of his suffering without her, and his wholeness when with her. He deeply dreads losing her to another lover. He dreams of her in her grave, and weeps bitterly. Then he wishes for a large coffin, carried by twelve giants, to throw into the sea. It will be very heavy since all his love and suffering will be in it.

At the Wigmore Hall in February, 1927, Mark, together with George Reeves at the piano, gave a varied recital of songs. Following songs by Schubert and Schumann, he sang four modern, Hebrew songs by Samuel Alman, which were well received: Min hag chadash (New Days, New Ways), Erets abot (Land of my sires), Eth kal liba masrahto (A woodland Idyll) and Al Eilah (For all these). Excerpts from the operas brought the programme to an end:' Don Giovanni 'by Mozart, 'Falstaff' by Verdi, Massenet's 'Werther' and' La Giocanda 'by Ponchielli. 19.

Predictably, Mark's social life in London was closely connected with Roger Quilter whose friends were mostly musicians or artists, including Lesley Woodgate, musician and secretary to Quilter, Wilfrid and Jane de Glehn(and their relatives, the Marshes) both artists, Percy Grainger, composer, Nora Forman, the musically accomplished daughter of a wealthy Scottish engineer, and Maude Valerie White, composer. Recitals were given in their homes to which some of the great and the good were invited and during which Mark, amongst others, performed. At first, Eva found them to be a curiously esoteric group, but probably less so as her English improved. She wondered, in a country seemingly with so many homosexuals, how the population increased at all! 20.

An amusing tale in the early days of Eva's marriage to Mark involved her inviting Nora Forman and Roger Quilter to an evening meal at their flat in Ordnance Road. She asked Mark what she should prepare for them, being unaware of English customs. "Oh, just toast and marmalade," he replied nonchalantly. Which she did, and which her guests ate without comment. This became a classic family anecdote. 21.

Fortunately, sooner rather than later, Quilter, enchanted by Eva's endearing personality, changed his attitude to her to one of affectionate acceptance. His fixation for Mark as a potential lover faded, and he moved on to other fanciable young men, usually secretaries. In fact, Quilter and Eva became quite close; she was able to confide her problems and worries to him, and he was a genuinely sympathetic ear regarding the sufferings of her family in Lodz.

Disillusioned by their financial problems in Palestine, and partly due to Sara's homesickness for the rest of their large, extended family, the Taglichts made the disastrous decision of returning to Poland, probably late in 1926, or 1927, since Mark and Eva were reunited with them all in Lodz in July 1927. Fabius Taglicht regretted having sold up to move the family to Palestine. It was a mistake, he said, and clearly their circumstances in Lodz were less favourable than before the move. 21.

Mark was shocked to the core by the grinding poverty and dirt of the ghetto, with so many people living in one room, and often still wearing the ancient dress of the Jews. His immediate reaction was to want to leave as soon as possible, realising that his own people had emerged from similar poverty and extreme hardship. Eva's family, though, were quite a different calibre.

Instead, he and Eva visited his stepfather's, (Hyam Wiseblatt) mother, who was living in misery, but who expressed only joy to see them and to receive their news, saying not a word about her own plight. Mark thought them to be darling people, but they all looked as if life was too much for them. He also noted that apart from police and tram drivers, Jews were the only people to be seen, keeping to the unofficial ghetto with little chance of improving themselves. 22.

It was not all doom and gloom as Mark was fascinated by the Chassidim of the Lodz area, singing psalms in Yiddish in wonderful quarter tones, and he felt very much drawn to them, to their music and their dancing. 23.

Chassidism, as a religious and spiritual movement, arose in Poland during the 18th century at a time of persistent economic stagnation and military conflict. The movement was derived from the Hebrew meaning 'the pious', and provided relief from life's misfortunes with ecstatic prayer on a daily basis, loud singing and dancing, a high level of orthodoxy and rigorous study of the Talmud and Torah. The spiritual leader of a group was known as a 'tzaddick', and pilgrimages were often made to his house where advice was given and prayers said or sung. 24.

Leaving Poland was very sad. Mark considered the journey and stay to be worthwhile, but he was anxious to leave dreary Lodz which Eva described as godforsaken. After meeting up with Nora Forman, during which time she gave them £50 of shares in 'The Teashop in Rome', they revisited Vienna with her, and then Salzburg, returning to London on 27th September. They were both glad to be back, and Mark had precisely £19 in his bank account! Shortly after their return, he received an offer to sing from the BBC, and also a cheque from a pupil which temporarily relieved him from the worry of making ends meet. In his free time he worked at counterpoint, giving thought to composition, which worried Eva since she feared he would neglect his singing, his livelihood. 25. With Roger Quilter, they continued to move in musical circles and met Elisabeth Schumann, the famous soprano. Mark contacted his old friend and mentor, Samuel Alman, and played for his choir at the Great Synagogue in Duke's Place.

Marian Anderson, the celebrated, black American contralto, came to Britain in October, 1927. As she was a great admirer of Roger Quilter's work, she wished to meet him, and sing some of his songs. She also intended to take lessons with the distinguished teacher, Raimund von Zur-Mühlen, who had been Mark's teacher since the days of the Jewish Education Aid Society. On her arrival, she was informed that Quilter was ill and in a nursing home. To make matters worse, after very few lessons, von Zur-Mühlen fell ill, and was unable to continue lessons with her. Instead, Mark, knowing Mühlen's teaching technique so well, was able to teach in his place Although Marian was very satisfied with Mark Raphael's teaching, she had travelled three thousand miles, and was disappointed at not being taught by the great man himself. Despite this, she gave a successful debut recital at the Wigmore Hall on 15th June, 1928, singing spirituals, accompanied by Joan Singleton, but also accompanied by Quilter in his own songs. 26.

Amongst other friends Marian made in London, Eva Raphael was particularly helpful to her. When, owing to her colour, Marian was refused entrance to Harrods, which in itself defies belief, Eva was able to vouch for her good character, enabling her to enter. 27.

Periods of no engagements and few pupils depressed Mark, forcing him to contact Quilter for financial help, and then unexpectedly things improved. He gained more pupils and the BBC contacted him to propose a Robert Franz week for 1928. Robert Franz (1815-1892) was a German composer of more than 300 songs, and contributed much to the history of the Lied. His songs were full of sensitivity, and much appreciated by Robert Schumann and Franz Liszt. 28.

A revival of 'The Beggar's Opera' at Hammersmith, involved Mark playing the part of Filch, and, according to newspaper reports, he was 'a distinct success; he made himself at home on the stage, and turned the drinking song into one of the big moments of music without sacrificing any of the noise necessary to the tavern.'

In April of 1928, Roger Quilter, Roland Hayes (a black American singer who came to London in the 1920s to study and make a name for himself), Lawrence Brown (a black pianist and skilful arranger of music), Mark and Eva Raphael all went to Paris, and had their photo taken outside the opera house. It was not entirely holiday, as Mark took some singing lessons with Henri Albers, a well-known singing teacher.

In May 1928, Columbia Records issued valuable additions to their catalogue entitled Hebrew-Jewish records. Four Hebrew songs, composed by Samuel Alman, and considered to be of high artistic merit, were sung by Mark Raphael "who shows a musicality, understanding and a sense of beauty of the things he is interpreting." The songs entitled 'Eretz Aboth', meaning 'The Land of Israel', became a test piece for baritone and bass in the Jewish Music Festival. 29.

Interestingly, Mark appeared for one performance only in 'Riverside nights' by A.P. Herbert and Nigel Playfair in June of 1928 at the Lyric Theatre, Hammersmith. Later in the year he sang Quilter's Shakespeare songs, folk songs and Schubert's' Die Schöne Müllerin' for the boys of Fettes College in Edinburgh, and was delighted with the reception he received. 'Die Schöne Müllerin' is a cycle of 20 songs for solo voice and piano, with poetry by Wilhelm Müller and music by Franz Schubert. It is the romantic story of a young miller who feels affection for a stream which leads him to a mill. He falls madly in love with the miller's daughter who eventually rejects him in favour of a hunter. In despair, the young miller drowns himself in the stream which has been his companion throughout the cycle. 30.

Mark also broadcast for the BBC from Daventry. He was constantly worried about money, and in a letter to Quilter he comments that his body is not troubled yet (unlike Quilter's), but his mind always is. The success of 'Die Schöne Müllerin' in

Scotland prompted him to perform it soon afterwards, but this time at the Wigmore Hall, with George Reeves accompanying.

When Eva travelled to Poland alone to be with her family in 1928, she found that her father was still agonizing over the move to Palestine, and her mother was yearning for the whole family to be together permanently. She felt guilty about her own happiness, particularly as she was expecting a baby, and her family's lack of it. She felt that England had changed her.

The arrival of Roger Bernard Raphael on 10th February 1929 was a great joy to both Mark and Eva, and they became quickly absorbed in parenthood. He was named after Roger Quilter, who became his godfather. Mark worried yet again about the need for money and more pupils, and that the flat was too small for the three of them. He insured his own life, and for Roger's education, hoping that the child would be musical, otherwise he'd be in for a hard time.

By March of the same year, Mark had acquired enough pupils to take a studio in Wigmore Street to teach there on Tuesdays and Fridays. A successful engagement in Brighton was followed by a Brahms week with the BBC. Roger Quilter was working on his light opera, 'The Blue Boar', and Wilfrid de Glehn was painting a portrait of Lady Astor.

1. Information from Jane Szilvassy, Mark Raphael's daughter
2. City of Lodz. Wikipedia
3. Letter of Mark Raphael to Roger Quilter 16th July, 1925. MSS70600
4. Palestine under British rule. Middle East Research and Information Project
5. Roger Quilter: His Life and Music, by Dr Valerie Langfield, p.72.
6. Letter of MR to RQ, spring 1925
7. Letter of MR to RQ spring 1925
8. Roger Quilter: His Life and Music, by Dr V Langfield, p.76
9. Letters of MR to RQ
10. Letter of MR to RQ September 1925

11. Letter of MR to RQ December 1925

12. Information from Jane Szilvassy

13. Letter of MR to RQ, January 1926

14. Letter of MR to RQ , January 1926

15. Information from Raymond Raphael

16. Letter of MR to RQ, January 1926

17. Information from Jane Szilvassy

18. The Jewish Chronicle, November 1926

19. The Jewish Chronicle, February 1927

20. Roger Quilter: His Life and Music, by Dr V Langfield, p.76

21. Information from Jane Szilvassy

22. Letter of MR to RQ, 1927

23. Letter of MR to RQ, 1927

24. Hassidic Movement by Rabbi Louis Jacobs

25. Letter of MR to RQ, 1927

26. Dr V Langfield, p. 72

27. Dr V Langfield p. 72

28. Letter of MR to RQ, 1928

29. Jewish Chronicle, May 1928

30. Letter of MR to RQ/ also the Jewish Chronicle 1928

31. Letter of MR to RQ 1929

pencil portrait of Eva Raphael by Jane de Glehn

pencil portait of Mark Raphael by Jane de Glehn

*Eva's parents with three daughters: Rushzka,
Anjulka and Eva (bottom right) 1910*

Eva before her marriage (c 1925)

Eva and her parents with Mark c 1925/26

Eva's university pass.

Chapter 6

Into the 1930s

Fortuitously, after the birth of Roger, Mark was invited to sing in an increasing number of concerts and recitals in the late twenties, and throughout the nineteen thirties. As he became known nationally from the radio and from his numerous recitals, the number of his pupils increased too. Yet his concern about having enough money never left him, as it was deeply engrained in him from childhood. Some of his pupils took ages to pay for their lessons. On one occasion when he was teaching a pupil whose mother spoke Italian and who was listening in the next room, he encouraged the young man to sing, 'Mamma mia, manca soldi!' (Mother, we need some money!) up and down the scale several times. By the end of the lesson, a cheque had been written, proving that a subtle, musical innuendo can work wonders! 1.

Always aware of his financial responsibilities as a husband and now, a father, Mark gave more recitals, singing Schubert and Schumann at the Wigmore Hall in May 1929, but with the added interest of including some popular Spanish songs by Manuel de Falla to his repertoire, with George Reeves at the piano. This was followed a month later by more Schubert and Schumann,' Kinder-Totenlieder' by Gustave Mahler and German folk songs by Brahms, as well as several recitals with Roger Quilter. 2. Mark was definitely against being typecast.

Maude Valerie White, the composer, was given to having her songs performed all over the world, but when she invited Mark to give recitals of her songs in Egypt, as he had done in England, he refused. It would have involved being away from his little family for one month. The wonderful 'Eretz Israel' songs of Samuel Alman, recorded by Columbia the year before, were sung again by Mark at the Wigmore Hall in June 1929, to great applause and success. 3.

Percy Grainger, an Australian composer, and Basil Cameron, conductor of the Harrogate Orchestra, had planned a short festival of British music in Harrogate on 24th, 25th and 26thJuly, 1929, involving three different concerts, with works by living composers and some dead ones. The Frankfurt five…Balfour Gardiner, Grainger, O'Neill, Scott and Quilter…together with Bax, Delius, German, Warlock and others, plus Arne and Purcell. The composers conducted their own work, and when this was not possible, Basil Cameron conducted. The first day was devoted to works by the Frankfurt five. Mark sang four of Quilter's songs… 'The Jealous Lover,' 'It was a Lover and his Lass', 'Weep You No More' and 'To Althea from Prison'. 4.

Quilter's beautiful song set to Shelley's words, 'I Arise from Dreams of Thee', from the Indian Serenade, was given its first performance at the festival. Arranged for the tenor voice with orchestra, it was dedicated to Robert Allerton ,a wealthy American philanthropist and a close friend of Quilter's from before the Great War. Mark begged Quilter to allow him to sing the song, but it was really too high for him, and Percy Grainger thought the baritone voice did not come through. Later it was transposed down a tone for the baritone voice. 5.

The press comment regarding the entire festival was mixed.

An invitation from Nora Forman to stay with her in Somerset during August, enabled Mark, Eva and Roger to leave their small, London flat to spend time in the countryside. Mark really appreciated the English countryside; he loved nature and adored the beauty of Exmoor. It seemed to him that the landscape caressed him at every bend and turn. Unwisely, he tried riding Nora's horse with near disastrous results, never to be repeated! Both Mark and Eva thought the hunting set very dull,with no meeting of minds or interest in music and art, but Roger was very popular, as he was with the de Glehns who were childless. 6.

By November 1929, Mark was on tour again to Berlin which he referred to as ugly, but thought the concert life and outdoor life were wonderful. There his concerts included more Schubert and Schumann, including' Die Schöne Müllerin', and they went well. His next stop was The Hague where the Dutch public all seemed to speak English, and very much appreciated Quilter's songs, to the extent that Mark's agent suggested that Schotts should send his music to the shops in Holland. 7.

Life on tour, though, proved to be not always idyllic. Mark confided to Quilter that it was nothing but rehearse, eat, sleep and sing; that artists, generally, experience intense feelings of loneliness at times, and, of course, he missed his little family. 8. Touring was not confined to going abroad either. Mark could be giving a recital in Hull with the BBC Orchestra one weekend, and then off to Derby or Exeter the next. In March 1935 in Derby, he participated in chamber music with the Pougnet-Pini Morrison Trio, Jean Pougnet (violin) and Angus Morrison (piano).A recital at the Lincoln Music Club on 12th February, 1930 involved a varied choice of music: Purcell's' When I am laid in earth', and 'I attempt from love's sickness to fly',' Folk songs of Brittany' arranged by Roger Quilter, followed by 2 Schubert songs: 'Du Bist die Ruh,' (You are my rest)'Auf dem Wasser zu singen' (In the middle of the shimmer of the reflecting waves)and Schumann's

'Meine Rose'. The Lieder was heard with particular enjoyment. Bruce Hylton- Stewart accompanied.

The coming of radio changed the whole scene of entertainment in general, but particularly with regard to music. It was no longer necessary, although preferable, to attend a concert. As a reporter of the Exeter and Plymouth Gazette commented in October 1938, 'The principal artist was Mr Mark Raphael whose baritone voice is well-known to wireless listeners.' Indeed, Mark's broadcasts of many and varied programmes throughout the 1930s testify to his ability and versatility; he appeared in a London regional programme in April 1931 with Violet Brough (viola d'amore) and Howard Jones at the piano. In March 1932, he sang with Alfred M. Wall (violin), Howard Jones (piano), and with the Brosa String Quartet. With Gwen Knight, soprano, in 1934, he gave a recital of Quilter songs accompanied by the composer at the piano. In November, 1938, a programme of gramophone records was broadcast in which Mark Raphael and Lisa Perli, soprano, were accompanied by Sir Thomas Beecham.

Apart from his great love of Lieder, and the many Quilter song recitals with various sopranos performing with him, in June 1936 Mark was involved in "Monsieur Beaucaire", a broadcasting version of the story by Booth Tarkington and the light opera libretto by Frederick Lonsdale. The lyrics were by Adrian Messager, with vocal input from Mark and a number of other singers.

Unfortunately, like so many other businesses during the Depression, the partnership of Raphael, Lewis and Silver floundered and failed, forcing Jack Raphael, Mark's brother, to join a large company, D L Ormstein, as a manager. He maintained a very good salary, nevertheless.

The number of Mark's pupils continued to grow, as did his recitals. In May 1931, at the Grotrian Hall, he presented more songs by Schumann in German, from poems by Heinrich Heine and those translated from Thomas Moore, followed by eight

Hugo Wolf songs, and seven poems by James Joyce set to music by E.J.Moeran. Joan Singleton accompanied him. 9.

The small, gardenless flat in Ordnance Road was becoming far too cramped for the growing needs of the family, so when young Roger turned two years in 1931, Mark contacted the Eyre Estate who owned substantial chunks of St John's Wood. Fortunately, Sean O'Casey, the dramatist, was keen to relinquish the lease of his home at 19 Woronzow Road, so much to Eva's astonishment, Mark quickly agreed to take it on without first inspecting the accommodation. Evidently, he was particularly impressed with the garden and the fruit trees! 10

As it happened, the house provided plenty of space. Number 19 Woronzow Road, in common with most of the houses in the terrace, had been built in the Regency period. A basement housed the kitchen, scullery, dining room, a larder, a lavatory and a coal cellar. The music room was situated on the ground floor together with the sitting room which served as a waiting room for pupils. Another lavatory was situated on the staircase, leading up to three bedrooms and a bathroom. An attic housed water tanks, and presumably trunks and storage. 11.

Mark was now able to give up hiring the Bluthner Studios in Wigmore Street, to teach in the comfort of his own home. In a house on three floors, it was necessary to employ a maid full-time to do some of the housework, particularly as Eva cooked, took care of Roger, dealt with pupils, answered phone calls and provided hospitality to potential pupils and agents. She also fulfilled an important role in coaching Mark for all his *Lieder* recitals. As a perfectionist, and no matter how many times he had performed these songs, he always insisted that Eva should listen to his German before each recital to ensure that his pronunciation was correct. When singing Fauré, he would consult a family friend, Alice Spanier, who was French by birth. 12.

The first maid was Irish and forever leaving the house in the middle of her work to attend Mass or visit the nuns, leaving chaos behind her, so she was quickly fired. The next maid, Louise, hailing from Sudetenland, was capable and more satisfactory than her predecessor. She spoke only German in strident tones, was older than Mark and Eva by several years, and claimed Hitler was a good man, until Eva put her right on the subject. Somehow she and her sister managed to avoid internment when war broke out, on the grounds that they were domestics. Louise stayed with the Raphael family until sometime after the war ended. 13.

The whole household revolved around the singing lessons, and, when Mark was teaching, the music room was sacrosanct. The music was virtually non-stop, what with the lessons, Mark preparing for his own concerts and recitals, in addition to his composing, and later on Roger's violin practice. Number 17 Woronzow Road was attached to number 19, and the occupants, the Lewis family, were very tolerant and never once complained; but they got their own back on Sunday evenings with their hymn singing! 14.

During the early thirties Mark sang in many recitals, including one with Daniel Melsa, the brilliant violinist, who had delighted audiences in Berlin, Paris and London, in a broadcast with the Bournemouth Municipal Orchestra. He also performed for the Jewish Ex-Servicemen's Memorial Service, broadcast from Horse Guards' Parade. 15.

Having persevered with his study of composition, Mark published two songs in 1931. One was entitled 'Sleep', based on a poem by John Fletcher and published by J Curwen and Sons of London. The second was a two part song called 'Slow Spring,' published by Boosey & Hawkes, and set to a poem by Kenneth Tynan. 16.

During the summer of 1932, whilst Mark stayed in London, Eva travelled to Poland to visit her family again, taking three year old Roger with her; it would be the first and only time that he would see his Polish relatives in Lodz. When writing to Mark, Eva told him how Roger was happily surrounded by the whole family to whom she felt very close...so close in fact, that she felt torn between leaving them all and seeing Mark and Roger Quilter again. As it happened, little Roger caught scarlet fever in Lodz, so the return journey was delayed anyway. 17.

In March 1933, a BBC broadcast on Quilter's music included two dances from his three act opera, 'The Blue Boar', written in collaboration with the lyricist, Rodney Bennett. Leslie Woodgate conducted it, and Mark Raphael sang several items: incidental music to 'As You Like It', some extracts from 'Where the Rainbow Ends' and 'I Arise from Dreams of Thee'. A few months later, 'The Blue Boar' in its entirety was broadcast live on two consecutive nights, 23rd and 24th October, with the synopsis in the Radio Times. Stanford Robinson conducted, and Mark Raphael sang the comedy role of Robert, the Duke's manservant. In the same year Roger Quilter had written Four Shakespeare Songs, one of which was entitled, 'How Should I Your True Love Know?' It was dedicated to Eva. 18.

The year 1934 started with great joy for Mark and Eva with the birth of their baby daughter in January. She was named Jane, after Jane de Glehn, the artist, who became her godmother, as did Nora Forman, and they both took loving interest in her in the years that followed. The birth took place at 19 Woronzow Road, and the physician niece of Samuel Alman attended and delivered the baby. One of the larger bedrooms became the nursery where Roger and the new baby slept, and a nanny was employed for about a year. Young Roger had been enrolled at the Montessori School in St. John's Wood, and at the age of five, had also started to play the violin with Salvatore Seilhi Santi as his teacher. Later on, he attended Selwyn House, a preparatory school in St. John's Wood. 19.

In the autumn of the same year Mark and Roger Quilter planned recordings of seventeen Quilter songs which were issued privately for the Roger Quilter Society. These involved a set of six records which were made in November and December at the Abbey Road Studios. The first set was issued by Columbia Records, and then individually at bi-monthly intervals, starting in autumn of 1935 and finishing in summer 1936. 20. Three of the songs were accompanied by a piano quartet, with Frederick Grinke on violin, Max Gilbert on viola, Herbert Withers on cello and Quilter at the piano. They were: 'Come Away Death', 'I Dare Not Ask a Kiss', and 'Take, O Take Those Lips Away'. 'Cherry Valley' was accompanied by a piano trio, but the rest were for voice and piano. Other recitals given by Mark Raphael included one at 1 Herbert Crescent, Hans Place, and also at the American Women's Club in Grosvenor Street in June 1935, with Reginald Paul (piano), René le Roy (flute), Orrea Pernel (violin), William Primrose (viola) and Lauri Kennedy (cello). 21.

A BBC broadcast in Derby on 29th June, 1935, entitled 'The Empire at Work' featured a recital with Mark Raphael and May Harrison (violin).The Hull Daily Mail recorded another recital of songs by Roger Quilter on 8th August, 1936 with Mark Raphael and Olive Grove (soprano), and on 4th December of the same year, chamber music was broadcast with Mark Raphael and the Isolde Menges String Quartet, and recorded by The Western Morning News.

In July 1936, Roger Quilter presented his light opera 'Julia' at the Royal Opera House, Covent Garden. Much of it had formed part of the Blue Boar, with the same lyricist and librettist. The opera was not a complete success, firstly because Covent Garden was not considered the right venue for very light opera. A report in the Jewish Chronicle criticised all the dull talk throughout the opera to be the fault of the librettist, as more lines were spoken than sung. A memorable tune emerged in the Waltz Song, 'Love Calls through the Summer Night', which was fully in the tradition of British light music. Mark Raphael did not take part in the opera, as he had done in the Blue Boar, probably due to his other musical commitments, though he did attend it with Eva, and was disappointed with the performance. They both thought the work unworthy of Quilter, but could not say so. By January 1937, Mark had been appointed choirmaster at the West London Synagogue in Upper Berkeley Street. 22.

This appointment represented regular work which would continue for thirty years. Following his early training with

Samuel Alman at the Great Synagogue, and at cheder, Mark was knowledgeable in Hebrew and conversant with the liturgy, as well as being a fine singer. His job was to hire (and occasionally fire) singers, in order to maintain four part harmony, and train them to sing the Eve of Sabbath and Sabbath Services, as well as at weddings on Sundays. In addition, there was also special music for the High Holy Days, Rosh Hashanah and Yom Kippur, and all the other festivals of the Jewish Year. At first, the choir sang the music written by previous choirmasters, particularly that of Lewandowski , Dr Verrinder and Dr Percy Ridout, as well as the traditional Hebrew melodies, but having caught the bug of composition, Mark soon began to write religious music of his own.

Over the years, his output was quite prolific, and now takes its place in the British Jewish heritage of religious music, and is still sung and played to this day. The West London Synagogue also played host to numerous concerts over the years in which Mark participated or which required his presence. One notable example in May 1938 was the performance of 'Samson', one of Handel's lesser known oratorios, by the choral group and orchestra of the West London Synagogue, with visiting soloists. According to the Jewish Chronicle report,' the choir especially was outstandingly good in the choruses, having a clean, distinct attack, and responding well to the conductor's baton. Mr. Mark Raphael, as the conductor, is obviously an excellent trainer, and deserves great praise'. Most hours of the day, Mark was steeped in music, in giving lessons, in practising, rehearsing for recitals, conducting and composition. 23.

From 1937 onwards, the month of August was spent on holiday with the family at Overshot, north Essex, guests of the Marshes who were relatives of the de Glehns. In addition to music-making there, Mark would spend time at Dartington Hall in Devon, singing and giving classes, as well as giving singing lessons in Cambridge. In November 1937, he performed at yet another recital, this time the Verlaine Song Cycle to settings by

Gabriel Fauré, and a group of Hugo Wolf songs. The Derby Daily Telegraph recorded a Lieder recital in August, 1938.

The political situation in Germany following Adolf Hitler's rise to power in 1933 with his armaments and anti-Semitic rhetoric was worrying in Britain, but agonizingly so for Jewish people on the Continent. From 1933 to the outbreak of war, thousands left their native countries, Germany, Austria and Czechoslovakia to find refuge elsewhere; in the United States, Great Britain, Sweden, Switzerland, Canada , Australia, South Africa, Palestine and parts of South America. Some countries were more generous in their hospitality than others. The catastrophe was that millions remained in Europe vulnerable to Nazi evil, and those who had chosen to flee to other European countries, such as France, Belgium and Holland, were still not safe. With hindsight, the abdication of the pro-German King Edward VIII in 1936 seemed insignificant in comparison with the darkening forces of destruction evolving in Europe.

Roger Quilter was interested in helping a number of refugees fleeing from persecution, including friends made whilst studying in Germany and Austria in his youth. This help would either be financial or in the form of contacts which would enable them to pursue their careers in London. Or he would shelter them in his own home in Acacia Road where he moved to in 1938, close to Mark Raphael's home. In that year, he found himself in debt. He befriended Max Rostal , the violinist, as did Mark: Heinrich Simon, the editor of the Frankfurter Zeitung for about thirty years,(a man of rare intelligence and a splendid musician), and Dr. Rudolf Stern, a Jewish scientist from Vienna with his wife, Hedda, as well as refugee children. 24. It was Dr. Stern who was made to clean the streets of his beloved Vienna, and told the Nazis that he was glad to do so.

Quilter was very much sensitized to Jewish suffering by his close contact with Mark and Eva, and offered financial guarantees so that his friends might gain safe passage to England, supporting them financially until well after the war. The cruelty of world events revolted him to the depth of his soul, and as a close friend of Eva, he was totally sympathetic to her distress concerning the situation of her family in Poland, fervently wishing that he could assume some of that worry onto his own shoulders. 25.

Among the many gifted émigrés who escaped the Nazis from 1933 onwards to take refuge in England was Helmut Ruhemann, the art restorer. He had been chief restorer at the Kaiser Friedrich Museum, in Berlin, where he advocated the use of x-rays for his work, a rather avant-garde technique, and the complete removal of varnish for cleaning pictures. 26. He came to live with his family in Queen's Grove, St John's Wood, very close to Mark and Eva, where much of the picture cleaning took place. He was also involved in the removal and restoration of The National Gallery paintings to the safety of Wales shortly before the war.

Regardless of the prime minister, Neville Chamberlain's assurances of "peace in our time", war was looming with depressing inevitability towards unknown and inconceivable terror in many parts of the world, following so soon after the Great War: the so called war to end all wars. Those, who, like the London émigrés, fled to these shores from Europe and certain death, became, in fact, Britain's gain and Hitler's cultural, scientific, spiritual and entrepreneurial loss.

1. 1 Memories of Mark Raphael
2. 2 The Jewish Chronicle, May 1929
3. 3 The Jewish Chronicle, June 1929
4. 4 Roger Quilter: His Life and Music , by Dr V Langfield, p.81
5. 5 Dr Langfield, p.82
6. 6 Letter of Mark Raphael to Roger Quilter August 1929.British Library
7. 7Letter of MR to RQ November 1929
8. 8 Letter of MR to RQ November 1929
9. 9 Jewish Chronicle May 1931
10. 10 Information from Jane Szilvassy, Mark's daughter
11. 11 Jane Szilvassy

12. 12 Jane Szilvassy
13. 13 Jane Szilvassy
14. 14 Jane Szilvassy
15. 15 The Jewish Chronicle, November 1930
16. 16 The Jewish Chronicle, May 1931
17. 17 Letter of Eva to MR
18. 18 Roger Quilter: His Life and Music, by Dr V Langfield, pp. 87 & 88
19. 19 Jane Szilvassy
20. 20 Dr V Langfield p.89
21. 21 The Aranyi Collection, British Library
22. 22 The Jewish Chronicle July 1936
23. 23 The Jewish Chronicle May 1938
24. 24 Dr V Langfield, p.94
25. 25 Letter of RQ to Eva Raphael c.1937
26. 26 Helmut Ruhemann. Jane Szilvassy and Wikipedia

Mark and Eva with Roger and Jane at 19 Woronzow Road c 1935

Mark, Eva, young Roger, Wilfrid and Jane de Glehn,
and Rachel Marsh (Wilfrid's sister) c1932/33

Chapter 7

The Lied

Mark Raphael's singing teacher, Raimund von Zur- Mühlen, the renowned exponent of German Lieder, died in 1931 at Steyning, Sussex, after recurrent illness. It was he who had instilled in Mark a passion for German Lieder, be it for Schubert, Schumann, Brahms or Wolf, and also a consummate technique. It was as if, on his death, the lieder baton was passed from teacher to pupil. Throughout the nineteen thirties, Mark gave numerous lieder recitals and concerts, as he had done in Vienna, Frankfurt and Berlin during the twenties. Among these, was a recital of Schubert and Schumann songs at the Wigmore Hall on 26th June, 1929, with George Reeves accompanying him. The items were, 'An die Leier'(To the Lyre) 'Der Liebliche Stern'(The Lovely Star), 'Nachtviolen'(Dame's Violets) 'Liebhaber in allen Gestalten' (A Lover in all Shapes) by Schubert: 'Ihre Stimme' (Her Voice)and 'Provenzalische Lied (Provençal Lovesong) by Schumann. 1.

In January 1934, Columbia issued a record of Mark singing, as a tenor, a group of Hugo Wolf's songs, translated into English: 'Night's Magic', 'Give praise to Him', and 'In Springtime'. Percy Scholes in the Columbia History of Music (volume 4) wrote that 'Mr Raphael has a capital mind for Lieder, but not a great deal of voice. This is characteristic of our singers today. Choice falls between good brain and small voice, or no brain and bull voice. I prefer the former.'

Mark presented a varied and challenging programme of songs at the Grotrian Hall in November 1937, accompanied by Joan Singleton; it included early English music by Ford (1580-1648), Jones (1575), and particularly John Dowland (1562-1626); namely, 'Since I first saw your face,' and, 'Now what is love?' These were followed by songs by Schumann and Wolf, folk songs arranged by Brahms and the Verlaine Song Cycle by Fauré. 3.

In April, 1938 he gave one of several performances of 'Die Schöne Müllerin' at the Grotrian Hall in Wigmore Street. A press report noted that 'the opportunity of hearing Mark Raphael give his all at the Grotrian Hall was not to be missed by anyone who loves Schubert'. Another report regarding one of Mark's recitals at the Grotrian Hall, states that 'without making any great pretensions to powerful tone, Mark Raphael can none the less convey a sense of power, because his voice has very adequate shading within its range of tone. He possesses also excellent control over the melodic line, and can sing a sustained passage without the least deviation from the true note. And yet he has a definite vibrato which is sufficient to eliminate the effect of monotony, without being so violent as to make one uncertain as to which note is being sung.' 4.

The Grotrian Hall, also situated in Wigmore Street, was used by principal piano manufacturers as a recital hall where their pianos could be shown off under concert conditions. Sadly, it was badly damaged during the Second World War, and was later demolished.

'Die Winterreise (Winter's Journey) is a song cycle for voice and piano by Franz Schubert, the second of two great song cycles based on 24 poems by Wilhelm Müller, the earlier one being 'Die Schöne Müllerin (The Miller's Beautiful Daughter), as mentioned previously. Both were originally written for tenor voice, but are transposed to suit other vocal ranges. Schubert himself set this precedent. His friend, Johann Michael Vogl, a baritone, as well as being a literary scholar and accomplished in the classics, introduced Schubert and his songs into many musical households in Vienna. .

'Die Winterreise', like 'Die Schöne Müllerin', is not merely a collection of songs based upon a single theme of lost or unrequited love, but is, in fact, a dramatic monologue usually presented in its entirety, and lasting for over an hour. 5.

A synopsis of the song cycle portrays the poet singing about his lost beloved, an inconstant woman who has now changed her affections and prefers another sweetheart. As the cycle continues, he sings of abject loneliness and longing for death. All the cruel aspects of winter devastate his solitary soul; the bitter winds blowing, frozen tears, numbness, torrents and snow. In the sixth poem, he weeps copiously and his tears fall in the snow. When spring comes, the snow will melt and flow into the river, and will carry his tears to the house of his beloved. He longs hopelessly for spring, yet his heart is lifeless, and her image frozen within him. He sees a crow which he thinks is waiting for him to die, but he just allows the predatory bird to stay. Finally, at the end of the village, he meets a poor, friendless hurdy gurdy man whom even the dogs dislike. Yet he carries on playing, and the poet decides to join him. 6.

Unlike the passionate decision of the young lover in 'Die Schöne Müllerin' to commit suicide by drowning himself in the brook, the rejected lover in 'Die Winterreise 'is more mature. He suffers, endures and sorrowfully awaits his death.

Interestingly, in' Die Winterreise', Schubert has raised the importance of the pianist to equal that of the singer, the piano rhythms continually expressing the mood of the poet. The piano also supplies the effects of nature as mentioned in the poems: the crying wind, the forceful storm, the water under the ice, birds singing, dogs barking, ravens croaking and the repeated sound of the hurdy gurdy. It is not surprising to learn that Schubert wrote' Winterreise' when in a deeply depressed frame of mind. Life had lost its joy, and winter was upon him. The mood of the cycle is sombre, yet deeply moving. 7

Singers of' Die Winterreise'are required to demonstrate a deep understanding of the cycle, and sufficient power of interpretation to deliver it.

Mark gave his first performance of ' DieWinterreise' in October of 1938 at Dartington Hall, near Totnes in Devon, with Max Oppenheim as accompanist. A month later,' Mark Raphael's 'feat,' as the press referred to it, was performed once again at the Wigmore Hall. A report comments; 'To present Schubert's Winterreise song cycle in its entirety, with no break except for the usual interval, at the same time approaching each song with freshness and conviction, is a feat demanding not only energy, but also sincere and almost passionate interest in the work. Mr Mark Raphael certainly showed these qualities when he sang at the Wigmore Hall last week. Miss Joan Singleton accompanied.' 8.

Mark had become so passionately involved with the Lied for the greater part of two decades, building himself a fine reputation not only as a leading exponent of Schubert in the 1930s, but also as a distinguished teacher, that HMV contacted him in 1938 to coach no less a singer than Beniamino Gigli. Evidently, by that time, the world-famous tenor had already recorded much of the operatic repertoire, and wished to sing some Schubert which requires a different, technique: the art of the concert singer.

Gigli was the least intellectual and most natural of singers who displayed heartfelt emotions in everything he sang, sometimes to the point of vulgarity, but he had tremendous audience appeal. Having made approximately 290 recordings, he had all but exhausted the operatic repertoire for HMV. It was German Lieder which remained, and so after some tuition from Mark, Gigli recorded *Schubert's 'Standchen' (Serenade) and Brahms' Wiegenlied (Lullaby) in German in September 1938.* His German was embarrassingly bad (9) but there were few who had a greater God-given voice. (10) His mezzavoce tone was limpid and wonderful, even at the age of fifty, for he sounded younger, but the interpretation was scoopy, schmaltzy and ultra- sentimental in a way no-one had ever sung Schubert and Brahms before…or since! Over the top, one might say, but audiences of non-connoisseurs lapped it up. The voice was undeniably magnificent.

In 'The Singer's 'groundbreaking series, Mark Glanville, author and opera singer, chairs a discussion on the singing of German Lieder.

"More schmaltz, more schmaltz!" my first singing teacher would command, as he urged my young voice through Schubert's 'Standchen'. Mark Raphael's singing dripped with the goose fat used in Jewish cooking that has become synonymous with heavy sentimentality, and was none the worse for it. He told me that Richard Tauber attributed his success to 'sex in the voice' When Gigli had exhausted the Italian repertoire, EMI sent him to study Lieder with Raphael, himself an eminent recitalist who had worked closely with Gerald Moore and recorded Quilter's songs, accompanied by the composer. Gigli's resulting version of 'Standchen' was an unorthodox reading, closer in style to a Neapolitan song than the one man tradition with which the world of Lieder was about to be hit, but who is to determine which approach is authentic or not?.

The encyclopaedic nature of Dietrich Fischer-Dieskau's legacy, where almost no Lied went unsung and core repertoire was re-recorded so as to conform to the great man's own changing taste, has created a sense that only his way was echt (genuine) but Lieder, almost more than any other musical form, requires a uniquely personal response in order to communicate successfully."11.

Interestingly, Mark (Raphael) wished to be remembered more for his Lieder singing of Schubert and Schumann, in spite of his affection and respect for Roger Quilter and his songs.

1. The Jewish Chronicle, June 1929
2. The Jewish Chronicle, November 1937
3. The Jewish Chronicle, November 1937
4. The Jewish Chronicle, April 1938
5. 'Die Winterreise,' by Franz Schubert. Wiklpedia
6. Synopsis of 'Die Winterreise' Wikipedia
7. 'Die Winterreise' Wikipedia
8. Letter of MR to RQ October 1938
9. Christopher Fifield of *MusicWeb International*
10. Raymond Tuttle of Classical Net 11. The Singer. Mark Glanville

Chapter 8

Joe

Whereas 1938 was a successful year professionally for Mark Raphael, its sinister portent for war and destruction could be ignored only by ostrich-like fantasists. On 13th March, 1938, Germany invaded Austria (the' Anschluss'), and at the Munich conference of 28th and 29th September of the same year, in order to appease Hitler and avoid war, the French and British allowed Germany to acquire a large portion of Czechoslovakia, namely, Sudetenland. Hitler took the rest by March 1939. In September 1939, the Germans invaded Poland which brought Britain and France into the war.

During the twenties Eva's cousin, Berish Taglicht, had emigrated from Lodz in Poland to Berlin with his wife, Sara(née Biderman), where they rented and managed a knitwear shop. Their only child, Josef, was born in Berlin in 1926. 1. Berish and Sara would have witnessed at close hand Hitler's rise to power even before 1933, years of Nazi dictatorship and the immediate legal actions against Germany's Jews. During this period 304,000 emigrated. Life had been made impossible for them. About 240,000 remained. By early 1939, only about 16% of Jewish breadwinners had steady employment.

These restrictions were comprehensive; Jewish children could only attend Jewish schools, and Jewish teachers were forbidden to teach German Aryan children; kosher butchering was banned and Jewish shops were boycotted. The Jews were disenfranchised, forbidden to marry non-Jews, prevented from gaining many forms of employment, including being expelled from the professions and from commercial life. They were forced to wear a yellow cloth star of David and to carry identity cards, even though many of them had fought and risked their lives for their country during the First World War.

From September 1939, the government imposed a strict curfew on Jewish people, and prohibited them from entering designated areas in many German cities. Logistically, this enabled the Nazis to carry out their unspeakable wickedness more easily later on. When rationing was introduced, the Jews received less food.

Foreign Jews in Germany were the first to suffer Nazi persecution. On 28th October, 1938, 17,000 Jews of Polish citizenship, many of whom had been living in Germany for decades, were arrested and relocated across the Polish border. Since the Polish government refused to admit them, they were interned in 'relocation camps,' a sort of no man's land between Germany and Poland. 2.

On 19th October, two Gestapo agents arrested Berish in his home at 77 Friedenstrasse and deported him to Poland, allowing him to take only his coat, hat and passport. Fortunately for him his passport was up to date, enabling him to go directly to his family in Lodz and not to a relocation camp. In the room next door, his son Josef was trembling with fear and pretended to be asleep, unable to say goodbye to his father. Sara and Josef were allowed to stay in Berlin, albeit temporarily. 3

Throughout 1938, the situation continued to get worse, and on the nights of 9th and 10thNovember gangs of Nazi youths roamed through Jewish neighbourhoods, breaking windows of Jewish shops and homes, looting and burning synagogues. Jews were physically attacked and beaten up, and 91 died. Seven thousand five hundred Jewish businesses were destroyed, twenty six thousand Jews were arrested and sent to concentration camps. This pogram became known as *'Kristallnacht'*(the Night of Broken Glass). The windows of Sara's knitwear shop on Grosse Frankfurterstrasse were shattered, the place ransacked and the furniture thrown into the street to be burned. The merchandise was looted by neighbours and previous customers whom they had considered to be their friends. 4.

Following *Kristallnacht,* the British government eased immigration restrictions and agreed to allow a number of unaccompanied refugee children to enter Britain on temporary travel visas, provided that private citizens or organizations could guarantee to pay for each child's care, education and eventual emigration from Britain. As it was not safe for British Jews to travel to Germany to assess the situation, the Friends' Service Council (a Quaker organisation) which had been working closely with Jewish refugee organisations, sent a team of volunteers to Berlin and Vienna to administrate the project. Their task was to draw up lists of children, fill out reams of paperwork, supervise departures and chaperone journeys. This involved bringing almost ten thousand Jewish children to Great Britain from Nazi Germany, Austria and Czechoslovakia between 1938 and 1939, and was known as *Kindertransport*. Jewish organizations and the Quakers, directed by Lord Nicholas Winton and aided by Frank Foley at the British Embassy in Berlin, were mainly responsible for the success of this venture. 5.

Realizing the extreme danger to her son, Sara contacted Eva and Mark in London begging them to invite Joe to Britain, to provide him with a home and to sponsor him with a guarantee that he would not fall burden on the British government. Mark and Eva had the funds to promise this, and needed no further persuasion, and so late in May, 1939, Joe was able to join a *kindertransport* train to Britain with 300 other German Jewish children, travelling from Hamburg to Harwich by ship, and thence to London by train. 6. The fear and loneliness of these children travelling to an unknown country, unaccompanied by their parents, cannot be overstated. Before his arrival, Eva had contacted her prosperous relative in Golders Green to help out financially with Joe's expenses, but he declined, and there was no further contact with him. 7.

Sara was then desperate to leave Germany to join Berish in Lodz, but was not allowed to depart until she had completely repaired all the damage caused to her property by Nazi thugs. Since the insurance money had been confiscated by the authorities, and she had insufficient funds of her own to meet the costs, her family in Lodz had to send the money, not only for the repair work, but also for the extra departure tax, which was levied on all Jews. She was penniless, but able to join Berish and her family, the Bidermans. They spent most of the war together in the Lodz Ghetto. Their dream was to join Joe in England, and for a short time they were able to contact him by letter, until communication became impossible. 8.

When Joe arrived in London, he could speak scarcely a word of English, but fortunately Eva spoke German and Yiddish, as did Mark, and also Polish, which would have been a comfort to the twelve year old in his initial adjustment to life in a foreign country where he badly missed his parents. The sitting room located next to the spacious music room, on the ground floor of 19 Woronzow Road in St John's Wood became Joe's room, and although his real name was Josef Taglicht, he became known as Joe, a member of the Raphael family, an unofficially adopted son of Eva and Mark, an older brother to Roger and Jane. 9

The unaccompanied children of the Kindertransport were placed mostly with families for foster care, in small hostels or in boarding schools. Many schools offered full or partial scholarships to refugee children, with additional bursaries towards clothes and books. Quaker boarding schools were particularly active in this work, and up to one thousand refugee children attended Quaker schools before the end of the war. British and American

Quakers were jointly awarded the Nobel Peace Prize in 1947 for their work with refugees and relief. Yad Vashem has now added the Society of Friends to its archive. 10.

The Raphaels spent August staying with Rachel Marsh and family, relatives of Wilfrid and Jane de Glehn, in the countryside of North Essex at Overshot Mill, Colne Engaine, as they had done since 1937, and Joe went with them. When war broke out in September, the children were picking blackberries with their gas masks on. A radio broadcast by Mark was interrupted for the outbreak of war to be announced. Everyone expected bombs to start dropping, and so rather than return to London, they remained in Essex until the following spring. It was a privately organized evacuation. This was the period of the 'phoney war,' and for the time being, the bombs did not drop. 11.

During those months, Roger attended Earls Colne Grammar School, and Jane, aged five, went to an infants' school in the same village. In fine weather they were able to take a short cut to Earls Colne by crossing fields on foot, but in the winter, floods rendered the fields impassable, so instead they were taken by road in the milkman's van. Each day the five year old son of Rab Butler,(the MP for Saffron Walden, later to become a minister in Winston Churchill's government and whose wife, Sydney Elizabeth Courtald, was heiress to part of the Courtauld textile fortune)was driven to school in a Rolls Royce complete with chauffeur. He was very envious of Jane arriving in the milkman's van, and wished he could too! 12.

It was thought best to have the children educated in boarding schools away from London, so Eva and Nora Forman visited a number before deciding that Bedales would be suitable for Roger as a follow up to Selwyn House, his prep school in St John's Wood. To the delight of his godfather, Roger Quilter, he was definitely displaying musicality, and making great progress with the violin, Max Rostal being his teacher. Jane was attending a private school, Campden House, in Gloucester Road, but when the bombing started, she went to Dunhurst in Hampshire, the junior school to Bedales. Later she attended Luckley School for Girls in Wokingham, although in the early years, when the bombing waned, she would return to London to be with her parents. 13.

Just before the war, during the final months that *kindertransport* was operating, a brother and sister, Ion and Areen Grandy, who were managing a small private school called Lancaster House, located at 21 Cumberland Park, Acton, London W3, decided that their contribution to the war effort would be to save two *kindertransport* children. Joe was one of them. The Grandies educated him without charge, and gave him free board and lodging in their house during term time. In the holidays he returned to 19 Woronzow Road to be with the Raphaels, and to Overshot Mill during the period of the phoney war. When the Blitz started, the Grandies moved their school out of London to Shiplake House, at Henley –on-Thames in Oxfordshire. 14.

At this time, Joe's father and mother, educated, secular Jews, were suffering the cramped accommodation, squalor, cold, starvation and brutality of the Lodz ghetto, and yet Berish was reciting pages of English poetry to prepare himself for life in England. At first letters were exchanged, until it became impossible. Back in England, Joe wrote about his terrible homesickness, especially at night, not only for his parents but also for Eva and Mark, feeling so alone in a totally alien environment. Areen took him under her wing, and he threw himself wholeheartedly into his studies, becoming a brilliant scholar. Areen and Ion later arranged for him to attend the Cathedral Boarding School in Hereford (though not as a choral scholar) from where, at the age of sixteen, on the strength of his academic achievement, he was admitted on scholarship to King's College Cambridge to read English. 15.

London in 1939 was very sad with so many young men in uniform; sandbags everywhere, barrage balloons to thwart the enemy, and gas masks having become part of everyday equipment. Anderson shelters were set up in gardens, and Morrisons inside. Londoners seemed to be staying at home rather than on the streets. At the London main stations the trainloads of refugee children already arrived from Nazi Germany, Austria and Czechoslovakia were replaced by Cockney children and others, packed off to the countryside as evacuees. For some, the destination was Canada on ships which would be attacked and sunk by German submarines in mid Atlantic.

At the entrance of Liverpool Street station a *Kindertransport* memorial was erected to commemorate the 10,000 Jewish children who escaped Nazi persecution and arrived in London at that station between 1938 and 1939, without their parents.

1.   Information from Dr Danny Taglicht (Joe's son) and Mrs Margaret Taglicht (Joe's wife)
2.   'The World of my Past' by Abraham Biderman, p.142
3.   Abraham Biderman, Mrs Margaret Taglicht and Dr Danny Taglicht
4.   Dr Danny Taglicht and Mrs Margaret Taglicht. Grobman and Landes
5.   Kindertransport Wikipedia
6.   Abraham Biderman, p.144
7.   Information from Mrs Jane Szilvassy
8.   Abraham Biderman, p.144
9.   Mrs Jane Szilvassy
10. Kindertransport Wikipedia
11. Letter of Mark Raphael to Roger Quilter, September 1939. British Library.
12. Mrs Jane Szilvassy
13. Mrs Jane Szilvassy
14. Dr Danny Taglicht and Mrs Margaret Taglicht
15. Abraham Biderman, p. 145. Dr Danny Taglicht and Mrs Margaret Taglicht

Eva's parents in Poland before World War 2

Joe Taglicht, aged 12, in 1938

Chapter 9

The War Years

In the summer of 1940, during the battle of Britain, fought over the Channel and the South of England, the population was in fearful expectation of a German invasion which, thanks to the sacrifice of those in the RAF, did not happen. Then from 7th September, 1940, until 11th May, 1941, many cities throughout the United Kingdom were heavily bombed during the Blitz, including Coventry, Hull, Liverpool, Belfast, Plymouth, Manchester, Newcastle, Southampton, Cardiff and Glasgow; but none more so than London. Each night hundreds of German Heinkels, Dorniers and Junkers of the Luftwaffe would follow the route of the River Thames to dump their bombs on the city, and particularly on the East End where the docks and industry lay.

During that period 20,000 Londoners died, 1.5 million homes and buildings were destroyed or damaged, together with numerous, important ones: St. Bride's, St. Mary-le –Bow, the Great Synagogue in Duke's Place, The British Museum, The

Tower of London, Westminster Abbey, St. Paul's Cathedral and Buckingham Palace, to name but a few. Children had been evacuated in their tens of thousands to the country whilst their parents stayed in the city, or were serving in the armed forces. 1.

Mark and Eva Raphael remained in London, as did Roger Quilter, who lived very near them at 23 Acacia Road, St John's Wood, and who refused to leave the city, vowing that" the bloody German bombing "would not cow him.

Three concerts in January, February and March of 1940 were arranged in the Barn Theatre of Dartington Hall, Devon, where Mark gave performances of Schumann's 'Dichterliebe', Schubert's 'Die Schöne Müllerin,' together with songs by Brahms, Fauré and Debussy, with Mr. Hans Oppenheim as his accompanist. Dartington had become a popular recital venue for Mark since well before the war. He would return there, and to Exeter, where in October 1941,he featured with other singers in the Festival of Art at the Civic Hall in 'Voices of Jerusalem,' written and accompanied by Shula Doniach. This song cycle was based partly on traditional melodies, with piano and instrumental accompaniment. 2.

His return to Exeter in December 1941 was to the second of the Exeter Philharmonic concerts at the Rougemont Hotel. An interesting report from the Western News highlights how Mark was constantly intent on enlarging his repertoire, in spite of being principally a lieder singer......"Mr. Raphael's recital was unconventional. He sang a group of six 'Songs of the Troubadours', composed in the 12th, 13th and 14th centuries, and four Elizabethan *songs*: 'Since first I saw your face' by John Ford, 'Now what is love,' and 'Go to bed, sweet muse', by Robert Jones. Bassani's 'Dormi Bella' and 'Posate Dormite' were particularly charming. The 'Dichterliebe' was exquisitely performed. Mr Raphael and Mr Jacobson brought out the drama and poetry with much imagination."3.

When the National Gallery had been cleared of all its paintings and other works of art to a secret place of safety in Wales, Dame Myra Hess began her series of lunchtime concerts there in 1939, involving many artists, both British and foreign. Her main motive was to show the Nazis that war could not prevent the performance and enjoyment of beautiful music, much of which was German. Tickets cost one shilling and programmes one penny. 4. Myra Hess offered her fees from these wartime concerts to the Musicians' Benevolent Fund.

Mark's first concert took place in the shelter of the National Gallery on 18th September, 1940. It was an entirely Schubert programme, embracing Alex Rowley and Edgar Moy on two pianos, followed by Mark singing numerous Schubert songs; among them, An den Mond, (To the Moon) Hoffnung (Hope), Im Fruhling,(In Spring) and Liebhaber in allen Gestalten.(Lovers of all shapes), accompanied by Norman Franklin. On 6th June 1941, he sang in another all Schubert programme with Denis Matthews accompanying. After the war on 13th December 1945, he gave another performance of Schumann's Dichterliebe, followed by five songs by Brahms and three by Hugo Wolf, accompanied by Phyllis Spurr. 5.

The last of 1,698 concerts at the National Gallery took place on 10th April, 1946, with a programme of Haydn and Beethoven played by the Griller String Quartet. The paintings had been restored to their original positions. 6.

Mark's weekly work as director of music at the West London Synagogue continued throughout the war, as worship required it, just as in churches and cathedrals, and in spite of considerable bomb damage in the rear of the building. He broadcast a programme of Mendelssohn's songs on the Home Service on 9th May, 1941, music of a Jewish composer which could not be performed in countries invaded by the Germans. In March 1942, the Shula Doniach songs, entitled 'Voices of Jerusalem,' with the composer at the piano, were performed by Mark Raphael and David Wise, violin. They were: 'Morning Song', 'Arab Shepherd,'

'Wheel of Fortune', 'Yemenite Maiden',' Bells in Jerusalem' and 'Hora.' 7.

In preparation for war, the Auxiliary Fire Service (AFS) had been established in 1938 all over the country to supplement the existing fire stations. Extra stations were rapidly constructed for the AFS, or their services were added to existing stations. 8. They played a vital role both during and after a raid, coping with many fires caused by the incendiaries. Mark joined the AFS as an air raid warden and was often on duty at night as one of a trio of Jewish musicians who patrolled St. John's Wood. Harry Isaacs, the pianist, was another. Certainly during the London Blitz, it would have been a nightly occurrence, and it was at this time that Mark felt the need to smoke more to blunt the edges of his fear and nerves.

Elisabeth Parry, who became a professional singer and who was studying with Mark in the early war years, often went for her lessons in the morning, and the trio would have been out all night working amidst the wreckage of neighbours' houses without sleep. On one such occasion, in the early days of her career, she complained, 'Mark, I've done fifty performances now and I am still so nervous!' His reply was, 'My dear, it is Calvary every time.' 9.

With her knowledge of five European languages, Eva obtained a job working at the Postal Censorship Office in London, translating for the government letters which might have contained information of a sensitive nature or concern national security. The work required not only a broad knowledge of languages, but also total confidentiality. Eva continued with this work throughout the war, and breathed not a word to anyone, not even to Mark. Fortunately for the family, Louise, the maid from Sudetenland, continued with her domestic duties at 19 Woronzow Road until the war ended. 10.

Whereas Roger, Jane and Joe were being educated in relative safety out of London, Eva's constant worry concerned her family in Lodz since communication with them was no longer possible. She knew that when the Germans invaded Poland on 1st September, 1939, Lodz surrendered after three days, the Panzer divisions having decimated the Polish Army. She knew few details concerning the situation of her parents, her two sisters and the numerous aunts, uncles and cousins of her extended family, including Joe's parents, Berish and Sara. Her persistence urged her to attempt to use some of Roger Quilter's contacts to bring her family out of Poland, but to no avail.

In fact, the situation in the Lodz ghetto was unimaginably wretched. Queues of thousands of starving people waited daily to collect their meagre rations, often fruitlessly, pushing one another, falling over in the mud, some never to get up again. As time went by, the rations became even less, and all food was weighed in grams as if it were gold. Starvation caused tuberculosis on a large scale, typhus and cholera, with medicines either non-existent or in very short supply. Psychologically frail people went insane with the agony of it all, were admitted to the Jewish Mental Asylum, and there they stayed until July 1941 when the 'Rolfkommando' liquidated all the inmates together with those of the Tuberculosis Hospital. The famine and the filth combined caused a very high mortality rate within the ghetto. The pipes froze and burst during the severe Polish winters, and when all the furniture had been burned, there was no heat. Many took their own lives. 11.

In the autumn of 1941,Chelmno had been established as a place of execution for the Jews of Lodz and the surrounding areas, being situated only 83 kilometres from the city and easily accessible both by rail and road. The method of murder preceded the mass killing at Auschwitz, and was something of an experiment. Victims were directed into 'Spezialwagen', or gas vans, which looked just like ambulances. When the motors were turned on, the carbon monoxide fumes were directed into the back of the vans, asphyxiating the trapped victims as they were driven to the Rzuchowski Forest where they were buried. Later on, the corpses were exhumed and burned to eliminate all traces of the crime. In that area of Poland called Warthegau,

330,000 Jews were gassed in these vans of which 70,000 souls were from the Lodz ghetto. This was just the beginning of the Nazi extermination plans. After a while the 'specialwagen' were considered inefficient. 12.

Although reports of iniquitous crimes against the Jews in Europe became known to the British government in 1942-43, Mark and Eva, along with the general population, were unaware of the *details* of the unbelievable horror taking place in Poland, Germany and the rest of Eastern Europe until towards the end of the war. Eva was constantly anxious to know the fate of her relatives, and Jane would often accompany her mother to the headquarters of the British Red Cross in efforts to trace them. A letter from Eva to Mark, dated 20th April, 1942, whilst he was on tour, reveals her attempts not to worry too much since the situation might be better than they had imagined, and anyway it was out of their hands. 13. At that time the extermination camp at Belzec had just started to function, but the news of it had not as yet reached England. In fact, in June 1942 the BBC, alluding to the Polish government in exile, reported the extermination of the Jews in the East for the first time. The news reached people in the free nations and those in occupied countries who were secretly listening to forbidden stations. The gas ovens were made official. 14

No matter how catastrophic the circumstances, life goes on. Eva continued to work for the Censorship Office, and Mark gave more recitals, including three concerts in French at the Wigmore Hall under the Auspices of the French Committee of National Liberation. He sang 'neuf mélodies pour une voix avec accompagnement de piano' by Gabriel Fauré. This was followed by a trio for violin, cello and piano (Opus 120 by Fauré). The accompanist was Kathleen Long. 15. In Devon, Mark performed with the Chamber Music Group, and accompanied by Hans Oppenheim, at the Barn Theatre, Dartington Hall, Devon, on 22 January, 1940. 16

Mark was also involved in concerts organized by CEMA: the Council for the Encouragement of Music and the Arts. In each of the country's civil defence regions, one each for Scotland and Wales, and ten for England, excluding London which was thought to be already adequately organised, cultural activities in the form of concerts, plays, opera and exhibitions were planned to provide each region with non-profit-making companies. Hence Mark found himself travelling all over the country, in company with other artists, to carry culture to the nation during wartime. One week he might be singing' Arie Antiche' and Quilter songs at Folkestone Town Hall with the Boyd Neel Orchestra, the next week in Liverpool, at the Crane Theatre in Hanover Street, giving a recital of Schumann's 'Dichterliebe', accompanied by Maurice Jacobson, in one of the Liverpool lunch hour concerts for city workers. The Cheltenham Gramophone Society of 180 members were immensely impressed with his singing, and wished that he would record more often. The president added that he had heard that Mark was a 'gentleman of means', and only sang when he felt like it! 17.

Occasionally, Mark's work for CEMA clashed with his duties at the West London Synagogue, as it did in December, 1943, when he was staying at the Feathers Hotel in Ludlow, but touring factories deep in the Shropshire countryside, miles away from anywhere; he found himself unable to return to London in time for the Eve of Sabbath service.

Mark had written and published several compositions in the years leading up to the war. Two songs in 1931; 'Slow Spring', a two part song set to a poem by Kenneth Tynan, and ' Sleep', a song set to a poem by John Fletcher. In 1932, he wrote a two part song entitled 'Gay Robin is seen no more', to a poem by Robert Bridges. This was followed in 1936, by 'Love on my Heart from Heaven fell', the words also by Robert Bridges, and in 1937, 'Lay a Garland on my Hearse' with words by John Fletcher, and 'Memory' set to words by W.Browne. Arguably the best loved of Mark's pre-war songs was 'The Lamb' published in 1937, and set to William Blake's famous poem. No songs were published during the war. 18.

At the West London Synagogue the question of reducing expenditure on the choir was discussed by the Music Committee, with Maurice Jacobson in the chair. Due to the war, and many members being away serving in the forces, choir salaries were being held in abeyance, and a rota of singers was introduced, replacing a full choir, with Mark Raphael and Dr Percy Rideout taking a slight drop in salary. In this way a saving of £300 per annum could be made. At this time, many synagogues, including the West London Synagogue, took on the responsibility of supporting refugee children, in large numbers, and appeals were made for members to support them. As expected, the money was forthcoming. 19.

Mark continued working with the AFS during the period of bombing by German Doodlebugs and V2s until the war ended, unless he was on tour. When the war ended in May 1945, the relief countrywide was ecstatic, expressed in street parties and much jollification, as it was in St. John's Wood. There had been considerable damage, both material and emotional. A bombing raid in April 1941 had destroyed Wilfrid and Jane de Glehn's house in Cheyne Walk, Chelsea, which sadly seemed to mark the end of an era since so many artists and musicians had gathered or performed there. The couple moved to the relative peace of Wiltshire. 20.

Quilter's house and 19 Woronzow Road may have been damaged by shrapnel, but remained standing, although there were a few near misses. The Grotrian Hall, in Wigmore Street, where Mark had given several recitals was totally destroyed, as was the Great Synagogue in Duke's Place where he had sung in the choir as a boy. The East End was almost demolished.

The war years took a heavy toll on Roger Quilter's health, although he continued to compose. His professional contacts remained, as did his close, long-standing friendship with the Raphaels who lived nearby, with Nora Forman and with the de Glehns, but he lost weight, his hair became very grey and he developed severe headaches. The recurrent bombing had shattered his nerves, but most of all the loss of his beloved, musical nephew, Arnold, when fighting in North Italy was more than he could bear. Worse still in August 1945, he was forced to submit to major prostate surgery, staying in hospital for several weeks. 21.

The year 1945 brought more information about the genocide of European Jews, and what was to become known as the Holocaust, but despite many letters written to the appropriate authorities, and exhaustive enquiries about the fate of her family in Lodz, Eva received no contact from them, and had to assume that they had perished - parents, sisters, cousins, uncles, aunts and friends. No news was not good news. Like many others whose relatives had been murdered, she carried the sorrow and survivor's guilt with her for the rest of her life. Nor was there news of Joe's parents, Berish and Sara.

The truth about the horrors surfaced quickly when the concentration camps were discovered by the Allies, particularly Bergen-Belsen, liberated by the British in April 1945 and later burnt down. Raymond, Mark's brother Jack's son, was conscripted into the army in 1947,and joined the 5th Royal Tank Regiment whose brief it was to prevent too many refugees from leaving Belsen and heading for Palestine. 21 The barracks were divided in two, the soldiers in one half and the remaining displaced persons in the other, but the gates were shut. The British wanted to prevent bloodshed between the Arabs and the Jews in Palestine, but it must have been heartbreaking for the displaced persons to be prevented from gaining their freedom in the 20th century, after the barbaric treatment they had endured, with the loss of tens of thousands of their relatives.

1. The Blitz. Wikipedia.

2. The Western News February 1940

3. The Western News December 1941

4. The National Gallery Concerts/Dame Myra Hess, Wikipedia

5. List of National Gallery Concerts. 18th September 1940. 6th June 1941. 13th December 1945

6. The National Gallery Concerts. Wikipedia.

7. The Jewish Chronicle. 9thMay 1941. March 1942.

8. The Auxiliary Fire Service. Wikipedia

9. Thirty Men and a Girl by Elisabeth Parry

10. Information from Mrs Jane Szilvassy

11. The World of my Past, by Abraham Biderman

12. The Lodz Ghetto. Channel 12 (Yesterday) television programme.

13. Letter of Eva to MR 20/4/1942 published in the Brick Magazine. Summer 2011. 13a.'Silent Rebels' by Marion Schreiber, p.72

14. The Jewish Chronicle

15. The Western Morning News.

16. The Council for the Encouragement of Music and the Arts.(CEMA) The Centre for Performance History, London

17. List of Mark Raphael's published songs of the thirties.

18. West London Synagogue Archive at Southampton University

19. Dr Valerie Langfield, p.103 Roger Quilter: His Life and Music.

20. Dr V Langfield

21. Information from Mr Raymond Raphael.

Chapter 10

The Post War Years

The war was over, the country deep in debt, and much of London and the provinces, together with parts of Wales, Scotland and Northern Ireland, had been bombed into ruin. Thousands were in need of housing and Winston Churchill had been replaced by Clement Atlee. It was a time of austerity, ration books, clothing coupons, utility furniture and making do. The forces gradually returned, and many to bombed houses, particularly in the London area. Working class people did not have home owners' insurance, and those who did discovered that their insurance did not cover bomb damage. War widows had to struggle to bring up their fatherless children on their own.

The CEMA concerts which had led Mark and many other artists to perform all over the country eventually came to an end, as did those at the National Gallery. Eva's post of translator at the Censorship Office had drawn to a close, and she returned to her normal duties at 19 Woronzow Road. Louise, the maid from Sudetenland, left having found another job.

Since there was no further fear of bombing, cultural activities began to increase. On 15th October 1945, at the Wigmore Hall, Mark gave a recital of three song cycles. 'La Bonne Chanson' by Fauré, 'To Julia' by Roger Quilter and 'Dichterliebe' by Schumann. He was accompanied by the great Gerald Moore. This was followed by a performance of Schubert's 'Winterreise', also accompanied by Gerald Moore. Then on 28th January 1946, also at the Wigmore Hall, again with Gerald Moore accompanying, Mark gave a recital of seven songs, based on poems by James Joyce and set to music by E J Moeran. These were followed by another performance of 'Die Schöne Müllerin' by Franz Schubert. 1.

At the West London Synagogue, organization of the choir proved challenging as the hiring of Jewish singers, particularly tenors and basses, was difficult. For a wedding requiring eight voices, Mark would sometimes have to conduct, sing bass and control the choir. In 1946 there were plenty of weddings! He also deputized at the organ when Dr Rideout was on holiday. 2.

The choir was considered to be an essential part of the synagogue services, but during the war standards had dropped, some singers had been serving with the forces, and others had aged. The alto line was weak, and therefore Mark suggested engaging another contralto. In his opinion, the seating arrangement for the choir was bad for both blend and ensemble, and he suggested permanent choir pews. 3.

By 1947, the choir numbers had been brought up to thirteen, with the desired number of sixteen. The idea was to familiarize the new people with the music and traditions, and later to encourage the old ones to leave, thereby reducing numbers to twelve. Then the choir would be fully operational. A number of other concerns were addressed, including the state of the music copies, the need to hire an assistant organist, and extra singers as an overflow choir for the High Holy Days. Having discussed the pros and cons of hiring a cantor, the Music Committee, including Rabbi Reinhart, decided against the idea and agreed that hymns in English should not be omitted from the services. Strong criticism of the music as unsatisfactory, both in content and performance, was vehemently expressed, as was the choir's lack of decorum. The excessive noise should be controlled, and the continuous coming and going during the sermon should be stopped! 4.

In August, 1947, HMV recorded Mark singing two most beautiful songs by Hugo Wolf, with Gerald Moore accompanying. They were both from the' Spanisches Liederbuch' (Spanish Songbook). The first 'Nun wandre, Maria' (Just wander, Mary) portrays Joseph's gentle encouragement to Mary, so near to giving birth whilst on their long and weary journey to Bethlehem. The second 'Herr, was trägt der Boden hier'(Lord, what does this ground bear?) is a deeply moving dialogue between a sinner and the crucified Christ. The Gramophone review noted that "singing so intelligent and deeply felt as this should commend itself to all lovers of the Lied. The balance between voice and piano has evidently been handled with great care, and the recording conveys a real feeling of intimacy."

On 9th May, 1949, at the Wigmore Hall, Mark sang groups of songs by Hugo Wolf, Robert Schumann, Franz Schubert and some 'Arie Antiche', accompanied by Gerald Moore. Ralph Hill of the Daily Mail described Mark as 'a superb singer'.

In early 1946, following prostate surgery, Roger Quilter's mental health deteriorated, resulting not only from the surgery, but from the agony of war and from the death of his beloved nephew. His chronic depression turned into a complete nervous breakdown, and his behaviour changed radically. He lost all sense of reality, his physical appearance coarsened and his homosexual appetite became uninhibited, increasing the chance of blackmail. Relatives would have been informed of his condition, and contact was made with the well-known mental hospital, St Andrew's Northampton, for permission to be granted for his admission. Some action had to be taken, so with a plausible excuse of some sort, Mark accompanied him to Northampton, without divulging the destination, where Quilter was summarily admitted, much to his bitter chagrin. Hospital treatment was necessary, yet Quilter was enraged by what he regarded as Mark's trickery. 5.

Various performances of Shula Doniach's music, with the composer at the piano, took place in the late forties, namely 'Voices of Jerusalem,' and also 'Songs of Sorrow' by Roger Quilter. Mark sang together with Nora Gruhn, soprano, and the Brainin String Quartet in 1947 at the West London Synagogue, with the BBC Symphony Orchestra in February 1949 and at the Wigmore Hall in the following June. 6.

Despite persistent letter writing and exhaustive enquiries after the war, Eva received no information about the fate of her parents and two sisters in Lodz along with her extended family, and so gradually she realized that they had perished. There was no contact either from her cousin, Berish, and his wife, Sara, Joe's parents. Having graduated from King's College, Cambridge, at such a young age, an achievement of which any parent would have been wholly proud, Joe, too, had to acknowledge that his parents were dead. 7. It would have occurred to Mark that had his own parents not moved to England at the end of the19ᵗʰcentury, the whole family would have been exterminated.

It is now well documented that at the outbreak of war the Jewish population of Lodz was removed to the slum area of that city, and by April 1940, the Ghetto was sealed off with a high fence and barbed wire, preventing escape. It was run by Mordechai Chaim Rumkowski, a retired 62 year old widower and director of a Jewish orphanage, aided by a Jewish Council which he appointed. He was also supported by the Jewish police and the Jewish *Sonderkommando*. Rumkowski was convinced that the survival of the Jewish population depended on cooperation with the Germans. In contrast to the Warsaw ghetto, the Jews of Lodz did not rebel, and in consequence, it was the longest surviving ghetto, but at a terrible price. Rumkowski set up factories to support the German war effort, and those who worked were paid in food, but they were forced to pay for their continued incarceration. The amount of food was minimal, and the people starved. Anyone disagreeing with Rumkowski was deported. 8.

In December 1941, the Nazis required 20,000 for 'deportation', and two weeks later they demanded 34,000 more, all to Chelmno. In September 1942, everyone incapable of work was deported: the sick, the old and the children. Rumkowski agreed to this. Since the German armaments division was desperate for munitions, the capable residents of Lodz continued to work, so that there was a temporary lull in deportations, but rations were reduced. 9.

On 10th June 1944, Heinrich Himmler ordered the liquidation of the Lodz ghetto. The residents were told that they were needed in Germany to repair the damage caused by air raids. The transports began on 23rd June, and by August 1944, the Lodz ghetto had been liquidated. Of the 230,000 Lodz Jews, plus the 25,000 transported in, only about 800 remained, left behind to clean the housing for the Germans, and to collect all the Jewish possessions to be sent to Germany. These 1944 transports were to Auschwitz, and Rumkowski and family were included. The Nazis had intended to kill the remaining Jews, but the Russians arrived sooner than they thought, and the Ghetto was liberated. Survivors, photos, films and Nazi records bear testimony to the monstrous events that had taken place. 10.

Several decades later, Abraham Biderman, a survivor not only of the Lodz ghetto, but of the Dora, Auschwitz and finally Bergen-Belson concentration camps, wrote a book entitled 'The World of My Past', recalling disturbing details of the years he spent in wartime Lodz. He shared cramped accommodation, starvation, disease and cold, not only with his parents and older brother, Lipek, but also with Berish Taglicht, his uncle, and his wife, Sara - Joe's parents. 11.

The Bidermans and the Taglichts were among the last to leave the ghetto in the August of 1944, and the destination was

Auschwitz. Abraham, aged twenty, met his uncle Berish in the camp, and shared a brief, emotional reunion with him. His aunt Sara was in the women's section. He never saw either of them again. 12. Years later, their son, Joe Taglicht, finally obtained conclusive evidence of where his parents were murdered, and registered the fact with Yad Vashem in Jerusalem. 13. Eva did not discover how her relatives perished, and never got over it. Her friends, particularly Quilter, Nora Forman, Wilfrid and Jane de Glehn and Tammy White, (the sister of the composer, Maude Valerie White,) together with Mark and his relatives, were of great comfort and support to her at the time, as were her children, Roger and Jane. Eva had a special bond of understanding and compassion with Joe.

Before the end of the war, Roger, dissatisfied with his violin tuition at Bedales, and after gaining an exemption certificate, left to study the violin in earnest with Sacha Laserson . He kept in regular touch with his godfather, Roger Quilter, who was delighted with his musical development. Jane left her boarding school to study at the French Institute, and then later at the Regent Street Polytechnic. She studied nursing for a time at Great Ormond Street Hospital, and then pursued secretarial work. 14. After graduating from King's College Cambridge, Joe spent some time in West Africa, studying African languages. 15.

It so happened that of the refugees admitted into Britain before the Second World War (approximately 80,000, excluding the 10,000 children of Kindertransport), many settled in North West London, so that when the war ended and the forces returned, many with no homes to go to, there was friction between those who occupied the accommodation and those who felt the returning soldiers should have priority. 16. In addition to this problem, amid the general post-war austerity, thousands of refugees were desperately trying to trace their relatives in Europe, contacting regularly the Red Cross, the Association of Jewish Refugees, the Austrian Centre, Bloomsbury House, Woburn House and the Quakers. It was an agonizing time for

Eva, Joe and all concerned, since for many, there was silence and the relatives were presumed dead.

Uncharitable groups in Hampstead petitioned for the refugees to return to their own countries now that Hitler was dead, and thugs exacerbated an already fraught situation. It was certainly not their finest hour. However, it should be borne in mind that, 'What is beyond argument is that Britain accepted more refugees relative to the size of its population than other countries, including the United States, which had a far greater absorptive capacity.' 17. Geographically, the whole of Britain was smaller than some American states...about half the size of Wyoming. A scheme for building many more houses, and repairing the bomb-damaged ones was put into operation, and the Home Secretary announced the British Government's new naturalization policy: foreign residents who had been in the country for five years could become British. Since the refugees had all arrived before the end of 1939, it meant that they were all eligible for citizenship. 18.

Unsurprisingly, many survivors of the Holocaust became agnostics or atheists. Where was God in Belzec, Sobibor, Treblinka, Dachau, Belsen, Belzec and Auschwitz? Why did He allow this barbarity and murder on a massive scale to happen? Were not the Jews His chosen people who had worshipped Him as their one true God for thousands of years? Why then did He not intervene? Others, knowing that human beings possess free will, a capacity for extreme evil as well as for good, realised that the Holocaust resulted from man's inhumanity to man, and clung to their Faith, hoping to strive for something better in the future. Others again, concentrated on making the most of this life in a material sense, without thinking about the next. Mark was clearly affected by Eva and Joe's loss, too, and in later years, when asked by a rabbi at the West London Synagogue what he believed in, replied," I don't know what I believe in...I believe in music!"

Sadly in 1947, at the age of 69, Samuel Alman died. He had been the dominant figure in Anglo-Jewish synagogue music during the first four decades of the 20th century, as well as Mark's teacher, choirmaster and mentor from the days of the Great Synagogue in Duke's Place. In 1916, he moved to the Hampstead Synagogue and remained for thirty years, living in Swiss Cottage. He sought to bring Jewish music to a wider audience than the synagogue, so he founded and ran two choirs: The London Chazzanim Association, and a mixed choir, the Halevy Choral Society. Both these choirs performed Jewish music for concert purposes, much of it was composed or arranged by Samuel Alman himself. 19.

Alman's opera, 'King Ahaz', remains the only Yiddish grand opera ever written. Most of his compositions appeared in two volumes, entitled, 'Shirei Beis Haknesses',(Songs of the Synagogue), published in 1925 and 1938. In 1946, having retired from Hampstead Synagogue, he was created Director of Music for the entire United Synagogue, a position which he held for barely a year. Mark, Eva and family visited him regularly at his home in Swiss Cottage until he died, and Mark later referred to him as being so talented in composition that 'he could write on a bus!'

During the late forties, Mark's reputation as a singing teacher of distinction became well-known in London and beyond, to the extent that he attracted the attention of Noel Coward, no less, and Ivor Novello. Their interest in Mark was not so much for themselves, but for their 'partners', Graham Payne and Jan Mazurus, who were intent on taking lessons in singing .As a rule, Coward would bring Graham Payne, his longstanding partner, to the lesson, collect him when it was over and pay the fee. On one occasion, Mark's teenage son, Roger, opened the door to Coward, and ushered him in.

"I've met your father," enunciated Coward in his ultra clipped accent.

"So I gather," replied young Roger, in an accent to match! 20.

Another interesting student, Abraham Beniso, a Gibraltarian, arrived in London to study not only for a teaching diploma at Jews' College, but also the ' Chazanut' which is the method by which a cantor sings the liturgy of the services. He became very popular at weddings and funerals. In 1949 he enrolled at the London College of Music where Mark was employed, and studied with him. Mark was impressed with his voice and advised him to audition at the Guildhall School of Music. He was accepted, and for two years became a cantor of Bevis Marks (arguably the oldest synagogue in the UK), and one of the most highly regarded cantors within worldwide Sephardim. Abraham was described as a tenor, but the extraordinary phenomenon is that his voice had never broken, and therefore at eighty years old it remained as pure as it was when he was twenty.

The London College of Music, where Mark was employed, was founded in 1887, and existed as an independent music conservatoire based at Great Marlborough Street in Central London until 1991.It then moved to Ealing and became part of the Polytechnic of West London which in 2011 was renamed as the University of West London.

Mark's acute hearing and experienced ear would quickly detect a pupil's vocal and musical strengths or weaknesses, and he would readily provide individual exercises to correct the weak points or enhance the strengths. These might involve sight reading exercises, the purity of vowels and the elimination of the English diphthong in favour of Italianate vowels, the improvement of high or low notes and intonation, the interpretation of the repertoire, phrasing and the art of breathing. The warming up methods came from the Vaccai and Panofka vocal exercises, providing melodious ways of combining all those points, plus the practice of vocal flexibility. Vaccai was particularly useful in that each exercise dealt with a newly-introduced musical interval, enabling the singer to become a better musician in the future, although clearly pupils varied in their musical achievement before beginning the lessons. Mark's sound grasp of French, German, Yiddish and Italian and his general linguistic ability enabled him to coach pupils in those languages without a problem.

Also in the post war years, the future of Palestine became an important issue. After the First World War, when the British obtained a mandate to govern, Jewish immigration increased significantly throughout the twenties, provoking Arab riots and massacres. Then, during the thirties, the period of Nazi persecution in Europe, thousands of Jewish immigrants fled to Palestine, including some of Eva's relatives, creating more fighting between Jews and Arabs. As the occupying power, the British were caught in the middle of this conflict, desperately trying to keep the peace. Consequently, they tried to control the number of immigrants at a time when thousands of Holocaust survivors were anxious to start a new life in Palestine. Terrorist organizations, the Irgun and the Lehi, turned their aggression on the British which culminated in the blowing up of the King David Hotel with considerable loss of life and injury. 21.

Diplomacy failed to reconcile the different points of view concerning the future of Israel, with the result that on 18th February 1947, the British announced their withdrawal from the region. Chaim Weizmann had already convinced President Truman of the justice of setting up a homeland for Jewish Holocaust survivors. Later in 1947, the United Nations voted for a partition plan. The British abstained, and the Arab countries voted against, but the majority of countries supported the plan. The British withdrew from Palestine on 14th May 1948, and David Ben Gurion announced the creation of the State of Israel, with the support of President Truman and the United States of America. After a diaspora lasting approximately two thousand years, the State of Israel was born, a homeland for the Jews, amid great jubilation.

1.   Wigmore Hall recitals in the forties. Jewish Chronicle
2.   West London Synagogue Archives at Southampton University
3.   WLS Archives at Southampton University

4. WLS Archives at Southampton University

5. Roger Quilter: His Life and Music by Dr V Langfield, p.103. Her recorded interview with Roger Raphael in 1997.

6. The Jewish Chronicle June 1949

7. Dr Danny Taglicht/ Mrs Margaret Taglicht

8. The Lodz Ghetto BBC Channel 12 (Yesterday) Television Programme

9. Lodz in World War 2. Wikipedia.

10. The Lodz Ghetto. Channel 12 (Yesterday) Television Programme.

11. 'The World of My Past' by Abraham Biderman, p.242

12. 'The World of My Past' by Abraham Biderman

13. Yad Vashem records

14. Information from Mrs Jane Szilvassy

15. Dr Danny Taglicht/Mrs Margaret Taglicht

16. 'The List' by Martin Fletcher, p.82

17. 'Jewish London: An Illustrated History' by Dr Gerry Black, p.154

18. 'The List' by Martin Fletcher, p.232

19. Samuel Alman: Dr Michael Jolles

20. Information from Mrs Jane Szilvassy

21. Post War Palestine Wikipedia

22. The Founding of the State of Israel. BBC News.

Chapter 11
The Fifties

Despite the harsh reality of the Arab-Israeli war of 1948, with its inevitable loss of life and injury, a sense of euphoria remained in Jewish Zionist circles regarding the new State of Israel which was expressed culturally, and often in music. At the West London Synagogue on 13th January 1950, the Avodath Hakodesh (Sacred Service) by Ernest Bloch was performed by the Berkeley Choral Group of 50 voices, and conducted by Mark Raphael; the first time to be performed in Hebrew in England. 1. It is a great expression of devotion of Jewish concert music, and was composed for baritone voice, chorus and orchestra .A second performance of this work took place on 20thJanuary, 1950. 2.

Ernest Bloch, a Swiss-born, Jewish American composer possessed the outstanding ability to visualise Israel in music, and through his reading of the Bible. Alongside the European Jewish tradition, he created his own unique Jewish style. Much of his music reflects Jewish cultural and liturgical themes.

Then the first of a series of concerts organized by the Jewish Welfare Committee took place in Adler Street, E.1 on 3rd November, 1950. The programme consisted almost entirely of songs by Shula Doniach, beautifully sung by Helen Kitay (soprano) and Mark Raphael (baritone). "There is a seductive quality about Doniach's settings of the Hebrew songs which admirably portray the atmosphere of the Palestinian (Israeli) scene, with lovely settings of psalms 121 and 150." Other "At Home" concerts concerning Hebrew songs took place in the East End during that year. 3.

The arrival of a postcard from Israel brought wonderful news for Eva; after having written so many letters of enquiry regarding the fate of her relatives, she had all but given up hope. Her sister, Ruszka, the pianist, had survived the war and was ALIVE! Some time before the outbreak of war, Ruszka had met and married a Bulgarian national, and went to live with him in Sofia. During the war she gave birth to a daughter, Ani, but sadly her husband died. After the establishment of the State of Israel, Ruszka and Ani left Bulgaria to begin a new life there. It would have been a highly emotional time of joyful reunion for all the family, but particularly for Eva and Ruszka, whose memories and tears shed for the loss of their parents, sister and other relatives combined with the overwhelming relief of finding each other again. Journeys to Israel and London were reciprocated, and the families kept in regular touch.

It is interesting that Jews in the sovereign state of Bulgaria were saved from the concentration camps. Although Bulgaria was officially an ally of Nazi Germany, some members of the fascist government, the King of Bulgaria and the Church were responsible for the huge public outcry at the time, causing the majority of the country to defend its Jewish population. Between 48,000 and 50,000 Jews were known by Hitler to exist in that country, yet not one was deported or murdered by the Nazis. This story was suppressed by the authorities until after the fall of Communism in 1989 whereupon the Israeli government officially thanked the Bulgarian government for saving their

Jewish population. 4. This protection of the Jews did not apply to those living in the lands occupied by fascist Bulgaria, for example Thrace and Macedonia. Over 12,000 were transported to Treblinka or Auschwitz, and gassed. Ruszka had certainly saved her life by leaving Lodz for Sofia.

Back in London, Mark was composing more music which he had been less able to do, certainly during the war years, and this time it was religious music, in four parts, for the West London Synagogue choir. The musical setting of prayers for an entire Sabbath Eve Service formed just a small part of a considerable output for the religious services. Unfortunately, Rabbi Reinhart, the senior rabbi at the time, did not favour Mark's choice of music, resulting in continuing tension and argument between the two. As in other religious institutions, the director of music resented the interference, and the rabbi considered that he was in overall control, which created an impasse, and frustration for Mark, continuing well into the fifties.

The Jewish Chronicle reported that on March 16th, 1951, at a Jewish Institute Concert, the singing of Schubert songs in German did not meet with the approval of one or two members of the audience, but Mr. Mark Raphael brought it home to the listeners that if they rejected German, they also rejected Heinrich Heine, two of whose song settings were sung. But above all, it was Mr. Raphael's sensitive rendering of the songs that could not but bring conviction to all who appreciated music.

Near neighbours of Mark and Eva, apart from their dear friend Roger Quilter, were Bernard Miles, and his wife, Josephine, also living in Acacia Road, their property backing onto the Raphaels' garden. They had bought the former St. John's Wood School in 1948, named Duff House, and converted the tumble down school hall into a tiny Jacobean playhouse, the first Mermaid Theatre. By 1951, Bernard and Josephine Miles had launched a four week season of opera and drama which began with a celebrated production of Purcell's 'Dido and Aeneas', starring

Kirsten Flagstad, Maggie Teyte and Thomas Hemsley. It was conducted by Geraint Jones, and recorded by HMV. (The dramatic production was 'The Tempest.') 5.

In that year Mark and Eva together with several of their musical friends, would have attended one of those memorable performances. Jane (Raphael),selected as an usherette for the production of Purcell's 'Dido and Aeneas,' arrived at her place of work simply by climbing over the garden wall! These short seasons of opera and drama continued until Bernard Miles bought the theatre in Puddle Dock, Blackfriars in 1959, although from 1953 onwards, the seasons took place at the Royal Exchange. 6. Numerous other musicians and celebrities, including Roger Quilter and the Raphaels, gathered regularly at Duff House for parties and receptions there.

The passing of the years took its toll on the friends Roger Quilter shared with Mark and Eva. In 1951, Wilfrid de Glehn (1870-1951), an impressionist British artist who had married Jane Erin Emmett, the American-born artist, after whom Jane Raphael was named, died at his home in Wiltshire. 7. He had been a great patron of the arts, and a longstanding friend. It was at his home in Chelsea in 1923 that Mark had given his first performance of Quilter's 'The Fuchsia Tree', accompanied, of course, by the composer. De Glehn's portrait of Roger Quilter is to be found at the National Portrait Gallery.

Quilter himself had never properly recovered from his nervous breakdown; in fact further treatment at St Andrew's had become necessary in 1951, and after five weeks, on his return to Acacia Road, St. John's Wood, he was found to be very frail indeed, unable to walk, and in the care of the Heatons, a live-in married couple whom he had employed since 1942 (and of whom his friends disapproved) were to take advantage of his incapacity 8. It was a sad time for Quilter in that all his brothers and sisters had died, as well as many friends, including Ivor Novello who died in 1951.

Quilter's health continued to deteriorate, and in September 1953, a few months after celebrating his 75th birthday, he died at his London home with his protégé, Mark Raphael, and Lesley Woodgate, another longstanding, musical friend, at his bedside…as well as the Heatons. His memorial service took place at St.Sepulchre's Holborn, the musicians' church, attended by hundreds of people, including members of his family, Mark and Eva, some members of Gervase Elwes' family, representatives of the London music colleges, of the Italia Conti School and of the Musicians' Benevolent Fund, as well as many composers, performers, writers, publishers and admirers. During the service, the BBC singers and Chorus, conducted by Lesley Woodgate, sang two of Quilter's religious compositions: 'Lead Us, Heavenly Father Lead Us' and 'Non Nobis Domine' 9.

In mourning the death of Roger Quilter, Eva lost a sensitive, understanding, supportive, generous friend of many years, a man of great culture. Roger and Jane would miss a caring and inspirational godfather and uncle. Mark's memory of their friendship spanned thirty years. In spite of an uneasiness in the relationship in the early days, due to Quilter's homosexuality , he would remember until the end of his life how much he had learned from Quilter who had launched his career as a concert singer from the first recital that Quilter had attended at the Wigmore Hall in 1923 to their successful tours of Austria and Germany; how Quilter had bought him his first recital clothes, the many recitals in which he had acted as Mark's accompanist; their recording of many Quilter songs, and the financial help received, particularly in the early years; the professional and social interaction, living as neighbours, and the depressing years of Quilter's mental illness. As Jew and Gentile, music had bound them together in lifelong friendship.

Mark's obituary to Roger Quilter entitled, 'The Man and His Songs' was published in Tempo,(New Series) Issue 30 (1953-4) p.21.Cambridge University Press.

'Quilter often said that he loved poetry more than music. The poems he set to music would form an anthology of some of the choicest lyrics in the English language, while a collection of those poems which he loved but considered unsuitable for music, would give us an insight into his kind and gentle nature. Evenings spent in his company were a sheer delight. He had a great sense of humour, exquisite taste, and he delighted in surrounding himself with beautiful things. Helpful to young artists and friends, his generosity was of a most uncommon kind.

His career as a composer was interrupted early on by an internal operation which kept him bedridden for a considerable period. It was during his convalescence that he thought of setting some of Dowson's poems. Four of these appeared as *The Songs of Sorrow*. Quilter set them to music of a profound sadness. *Passing Dreams,* the most poignant, is of the quality one associates with 'Lieder'.

His melodies flow easily and without violence. Tennyson's *Now Sleeps the Crimson Petal* comes to life with unfailing grace and warmth. Shelley's *Love's Philosophy* pulsates 'with a sweet emotion'. The melodic line in Blake's *Dream Valley* flows gently on, as if in a trance. Correct verbal accents, phrasing and word painting, all had to fall in with his idea of 'keeping the line'. That is why his songs are attractive to singers who know how to combine legato singing with eloquent articulation. *Weep You No More, Cherry Valley and Autumn Evening* are instances where melody and eloquence are perfectly blended.

He is rhythmically kind to both singers and audiences, who enjoy the throbbing urge of *Over the Land is April* and the acid lilt of *Blow, Blow, thou Winter Wind*. The' tessitura' of his melodies is most accommodating for both the professional and amateur singer.

His harmony, counterpoint and decorative figuration are most effective, pianistic and individual. Play the opening bars of almost any of his songs and you are left in no doubt as to who wrote them. As with his melodies, harmonic progressions rarely soar into strange spheres. When they do, I find them very telling. In *Autumn Evening,* for example, on the words 'the breath of autumn evening chills,' the change of mood momentarily creates an icy tenseness.

His accompaniments, harmonically fragrant, sweetly lyrical and rhythmically interesting, are a joy to all sensitive pianists.

His work has had a most marked influence on contemporary song writers. Peter Warlock once sent him a song of his on which he had written: "If it were not for the songs of Roger Quilter, there would have been no Peter Warlock".

His favourite song-writers were Schubert and Schumann, but in his lighter moods he delighted in playing Strauss waltzes and Neapolitan folk-songs.

Roger Quilter wrote no symphonies, but in thinking of *Come Away Death, Fear No More, It was a Lover and His Lass, Go Lovely Rose, Fuchsia Tree* and many others, I should like to end with the words of the poet, Heyse, immortalised by Hugo Wolf: "Auch kleine Dinge konnen uns entzucken." (Even small things can send us into raptures.)'

When Joe (Taglicht) returned to London from studying West African languages, also in 1951, he decided to emigrate to Israel, where he would have been inducted into a course of Hebrew, and later served his time in the army. He would have made contact with Ruszka (and Ani) who had become the pianist repetiteur of the Tel Aviv Opera Company, and with relatives of his who had survived World War 2 by emigrating to Palestine in the twenties and thirties. He certainly kept in regular touch with Mark, Eva, Jane and Roger, as well as with Ion and Areen Grandy, his teachers when he first arrived in England in 1939, and with the other boy in their care. Whilst in the army, he met Margaret Stern whom he married in 1956. After completing his army service, he joined the English Department at the Hebrew University in Jerusalem, and in 1957, was sent to Oxford to pursue his D Phil studies, his thesis being on Middle English. After obtaining his doctorate, he returned to Israel and continued his work at the Hebrew University of Jerusalem until his retirement in 1993. He and Margaret raised three sons, Yuval, Daniel and Raphael.

Yetta, Mark's mother, had moved out of the East End to Westcliff on Sea where with Hyman she ran a boarding house, but they later moved back to a flat in Stamford Hill, North London, a few years before the war, close to their daughter, Kitty and family. Hyman worked as a presser for his son-in-law who provided him with work for as long as he wanted it, and they spent a relatively comfortable life, near family and friends. Sadly, Yetta developed cancer, and died in 1952. Her husband, Hyman Wiseblatt, died in the mid fifties.

In 1953, Coronation Year, a joint Coronation service of the congregations of the Association of Synagogues in Great Britain was held at the West London Synagogue, Upper Berkeley Street, W.1. The sermon was preached by Dr Harold Reinhart, senior minister of the West London Synagogue. The WLS choir was under the direction of Mark Raphael, and was supported by a children's choir conducted by Mr. Thomas Rajna. Mr. Arnold Richardson was the organist. 10.

In fact, Arnold Richardson, an eminent musician, became deputy organist in the later years of Dr. Percy Rideout's service to the synagogue, and took over when he retired. It was extremely difficult to find organists of the Jewish faith. In November 1954, Raphael and Richardson collaborated with choir and organ for the celebration of Dr Rideout's jubilee as organist to the West London Synagogue with a private recording of 'Adonai Malach' (God reigns Psalm 93) and' Kedushah' (Holiness). Earlier in the year, Mark was involved in a concert at the Stern Hall in Seymour Place, entitled 'Music of the Jews', which included liturgical pieces, folk songs and modern work, with the participation of Shula Doniach, M O Rothmuller and others. 11. Dr Rideout finally retired in 1955, and sadly died in 1956.

Mark continued to attract new pupils. Isabelle Lucas, a black actress born in Toronto, came to London to make her way in the theatre in 1954 and studied singing with Mark. Her first West End appearance was in 'The Jazz Train' at the Piccadilly Theatre in April 1955. She went on to stardom. .

In February of 1955, the state of synagogue music was put to a musical brains trust held at the Anglo-Israeli Club. The panel included Dr. Mosco Carner, the musicologist and conductor, Mr Herzl Goldbloom, singer of Jewish songs, Mr H C Stevens, music critic of the Jewish Chronicle and Mr Mark Raphael, the lieder singer. Mark Raphael, most likely reacting to his musical disagreements with Rabbi Reinhart, claimed that the state of choral music in most synagogues was rather mediocre. As soon as one tried to introduce anything of artistic value it was resented, and congregants always wanted the same old tunes. While congregations should have their own tunes for certain hymns, such as 'Adon Olam'(Eternal Lord) and Ein Keloheinu,(There is none like our God), he said a good part should be left to individual composers who should be inspired to write. Perhaps then things would improve! 12.

The happy occasion of Jane's marriage to Laszlo Szilvassy, artist, also took place in 1955, to which all the relatives were invited as well as close family friends, and colleagues from the Ballet Rambert where she had been acting as secretary to the company. To the delight of Mark and Eva, Jane gave birth to their first grandchild, Alexandra, in the following year.

During the fifties, Roger (Raphael) had received tuition from a number of influential musicians including the composer Matyas Seiber, and André Gertler at the Brussels Conservatoire where he was awarded the Premier Prix for violin and chamber music, and the Diplôme Supérieur for violin. On his return to London, he joined the Pro Musica Quartet and founded his own ensemble which was appointed as Quartet in Residence to Radio Eireann in 1959, and led to more than 200 recordings.

A large audience attended the Samuel Alman Memorial concert which took place at Adolph Tuck Hall on 29th March, 1957...ten years after the composer's death. It was agreed that apart from his string quartet which should certainly be brought out of obscurity, most charming of all were his songs, some of which have a quality similar to English folk-songs. Others have a slightly oriental colouring, and his arrangements of Yiddish folk songs are delightfully good humoured. The artists were Jacqueline Delman, soprano; Mark Raphael, baritone; Vivian Joseph, 'cello; Israel Hoffman, piano. The quartet Pro Musica, and a mixed choir were conducted by Mark Raphael. 13.

Zimra Ornatt, an Israeli soprano, teacher and composer who lived in London for some years, gave a concert at the Ben Uri Gallery on 8th February, 1957. In her varied programme, she sang old Italian melodies, German Lieder and operatic arias, but also included 2 songs by Mark Raphael 'which are worth hearing more often.' 14.

The Society of Jews and Christians held their annual meeting on 1st November, 1957 at Kings Weigh House, Binney Street, W 1. Professor Raphael Powell gave a talk to a large audience entitled, 'On Being a Jew'. This was followed by lectures in early music in both the Jewish and Christian liturgies. Mr. Mark Raphael, the choirmaster of the West London Synagogue, speaking of Jewish liturgical responses such as 'Amen' and 'Hallelujah', explained that after the destruction of the Temple (CE 70), all playing and singing were banned, even at weddings...but to facilitate the memorising of the texts, chanting was allowed. The development of the chazanut (Jewish liturgy) from early times until the present day was also illustrated by Mark Raphael. Mr E H Worrall, lecturer in music at King's College, London, spoke on early Christian liturgical music. 15.

Rabbi Reinhart took the unprecedented decision to leave the West London Synagogue in 1957 to become the first minister of the Westminster Synagogue, taking no less than 80 members of the congregation with him. His reasons for leaving so dramatically are not entirely clear. One objection of his was an increasing move of some leading members away from religion and towards financial concerns.

Few of the Council attended synagogue services, and he felt that their Jewishness was too worldly. It would be true to say that the synagogue was split in two. Rabbi Reinhart was approaching retirement age, and his contract was up for renewal. Some of the Synagogue Council wanted new blood, a younger man, and did not want to renew his contract which greatly distressed him. Mark would have been relieved at his departure, which concluded their ongoing disagreements. 16.

It was also evident that Rabbi Reinhart and his assistant, Rabbi Cassell, did not favour the renewed appointment of Rev Alan Miller as part-time Youth Education Officer, and they felt that they alone should be responsible for the spiritual and educational work of the synagogue. In the end, Rabbi Miller became minister of the South-West Essex Synagogue, and Rabbi Cassell went to a reform synagogue in Bulawayo.

In 1958 Rabbi Reinhart's replacement as senior minister at the West London Synagogue was Rabbi Van Der Zyl who came to this country in 1939 from Germany, during the war was interned on the Isle of Man with his family. Having witnessed the burning of so many synagogues in Berlin, he resolved later on to found the Leo Baeck College for rabbis in London. 17.

An article in the Jewish Chronicle, written by S.D.Temkin on 5th December, 1958 expressed great sympathy and understanding for Mark's position with regard to improving the state of synagogue music. He wrote:

'...Variants from the accepted favourites there are, and they should be explored. There is a whole corpus of Sephardi music, and modern composers have been busy here and in America. Samuel Alman's compositions have won appreciation. Less well known are those of Dr. Percy Rideout. Although not a Jew, he appears to have found himself in synagogue music, and in addition to great tenderness of feeling showed equal respect for the Hebrew text. His colleague, Mark Raphael, has composed so much music for the synagogue where he is choirmaster that the wardens have been known to ask, "Are we having a Raphaelite or a pre-Raphaelite service today?"

Choirmasters and composers should not be too despondent. Their efforts may be received with disdain, but surely not more than greeted the Psalmist when he bade the people, "Sing unto the Lord a new song". And it is the Psalmist's lyric that has endured, not the shafts of the grumblers.'

Interestingly, at a Christian-Jewish study weekend at Our Lady of Zion in W.11, the Reverend Edmund Hill presided over the study of Jewish and Christian prayer and ritual. It was considered to be of inestimable value. Mark Raphael, the choirmaster of the West London Synagogue gave a talk on 'Early Jewish Music'.

By 1959 Roger Raphael had assisted in founding Radio Eirann in Dublin, and Jane had given birth to her second baby, Nadia; a sister for Alexandra. Mark suffered a heart attack in that year which mercifully was a mild one and from which he totally recovered; a warning, nevertheless.

1.   West London Synagogue Archives
2.   Jewish Chronicle January, 1950
3.   Jewish Chronicle November 1950
4.   Beyond Hitler's Grasp by Michael Bar-Zohar
5.   Wikipedia
6.   Wikipedia
7.   Roger Quilter His Life and Music, by Dr.Valerie Langfield
8.   Roger Quilter His Life and Music by Dr. Valerie Langfield
9.   Roger Quilter His Life and Music by Dr. Valerie Langfield
10. WLS Archives
11. WLS Archives
12. Jewish Chronicle February 1955
13. Jewish Chronicle March 1957
14. JC February 1957
15. JC November, 1957
16. WLS Archives
17. WLS Archives

Chapter 12

The Sixties

Mark celebrated his 60th birthday in April of 1960, and, during the same year, the wedding of his son, Roger, to Irene Russell, an Irish pianist, whom he had met in Dublin whilst working for Radio Eirann. They were married at St Finbar's Church of Ireland Cathedral in Cork. During the service, Nancy Carne, soprano, whose husband was an old school friend of Mark and also a recording executive at EMI, sang two songs, one of which was 'The Lamb', published in 1937. The other was almost certainly, 'Love on my heart from heaven fell', published in 1936. In due course, a son was born to Irene and Roger, who was named after his grandfather.1.

Sometime in the early sixties, the authorities at the Eyre Estate in St. John's Wood, decided to demolish the terrace of houses in Woronzow Road, which were considered irreparable. This meant that Mark and Eva had to be rehoused. Fortunately for them, their new address was nearby at 17 St John's Wood Terrace: a delightful Regency cottage of great charm, though moving the grand piano must have presented a challenge! It was considered wiser to demolish that terrace of houses in Woronzow Road than renovate them. When it was completed, Georg Solti, the famous conductor, bought number 19. 2.

In 1961, Mark was invited to become a professor of singing and voice production at the Royal College of Music in South Kensington. It was an appointment which delighted him. His experience at the London College of Music, empathy with young people, knowledge of vocal repertoire and languages, musicianship, passion for music and superb teaching ability, quickly made him a great success.

He taught at the College three days a week: Mondays, Wednesdays and Fridays. On Tuesdays and Thursdays, he taught privately at home, and sometimes on Saturday afternoons. Friday evenings and Saturday mornings were, of course, devoted to the West London Synagogue services, sometimes involving rehearsals and the introduction of new pieces. Jewish weddings took place on Sunday afternoons, creating for him a very busy life indeed. He seemed to thrive on it and not to tire easily, in spite of his heart attack in 1959. Very little time was spent watching television! He was constantly busy writing new songs, or settings for the synagogue. Occasionally on Saturday evenings, he and Eva would invite relatives, old friends or private pupils to dinner, or be invited to the home of one or other of Mark's relatives.

The West London Synagogue, built in Byzantine style by Davis and Emanuel in 1870, and situated in Upper Berkeley Street, has a plain exterior; the interior, in contrast, is ornate, spacious and splendid, with a vast, domed ceiling lined with gilded mosaics. The highly decorated design of the choir and screen is set above the Ark with open lattice doors, and at the opposite end is a bronzed ladies' gallery, unusual in a Reform synagogue. Other large rooms for study, conference and hospitality adjoin the synagogue. 3.

The reason for the break with Orthodoxy in the 1840s arose from the length of the services, the sermons being in Hebrew and from lack of decorum. Although the men wear kippahs (skull caps) and tallit (prayer shawls), they are not necessarily separated from the women during the services as in Orthodox synagogues, the Reform movement of Judaism in Britain, combining both Sephardi and Ashkenazi Jews, having broken away from the Bevis Marks Synagogue in 1841. 4.

A large wooden screen, decorated with carvings, separates the congregation from the organist, choirmaster and the choir; but to some extent the congregants are visible to the singers, especially those sitting in the front row. The organist, Arnold Richardson, with his back to the screen, was well able to see Mark Raphael's conducting; the latter stood or sat in an elevated area facing the screen, as did the choir members surrounding him: three sopranos and two basses on his right, two tenors and three altos on his left. From this position, the voices could be heard clearly on the congregational side of the screen. Sometimes additional singers were invited to sing the High Holy Day services.

In the sixties, the four manual organ with its 57 stops was an impressive instrument, and some years before, had been tonally reconstructed by Harrison and Harrison. The West London Synagogue was the only British synagogue with an integrated pipe organ. Arnold Richardson was certainly master of it which was particularly evident in the voluntaries concluding the services.

The repertoire of vocal music for the services represented a mixture of the traditional, and works by Dr Percy Rideout, Samuel Alman, Lewandowski, Dr Verrinder, Mark Raphael and other choirmasters. In addition to the Sabbath Eve and Sabbath services, on Sunday afternoons there could be two or three weddings, or no weddings at all, fewer in winter. Many were prosperous affairs, as one would expect in London W.1. Quite apart from the glamorous regalia of the brides and bridesmaids, the ladies often wore full length gowns in mostly pastel shades with matching plumes in their hair, and looked very fine indeed. The whole atmosphere was usually one of vibrant, relaxed jubilation, climaxing with a joyful 'Mazul Tov,' to the happy couple. Very often, the reception took place in accommodation provided by the synagogue.

The choir members followed a rota in singing for weddings since only one singer was required for each voice part, forming a quartet, with Mark conducting. With reduced numbers, fortissimo singing was advised most of the time so that the choir could be heard clearly on the other side of the screen. After perhaps three weddings in sequence, thirsty choir members would sometimes gravitate to Lyons Corner house for tea afterwards.

During the early sixties, Mark's difficulty in auditioning new Jewish singers when those in the choir moved away or retired became even more frustrating. After 1961 he was able to fill these vacancies from a plethora of hard-up, non-Jewish musicians studying at the Royal College of Music. The result was a fifty/fifty split of Jews and Gentiles. The sopranos and basses were Jewish, the tenors and altos non-Jewish, but a great deal of friendly humour and joy of singing together was evident. The newcomers were already musically literate, and fortunately for them, they were not expected to learn Hebrew, simply to pronounce it phonetically; sometimes in rehearsal Mark translated certain sacred phrases for their benefit. It was quickly discovered that perfectly respectable words in Hebrew had the same sounds as rather less respectable ones in English! Giggles had to be suppressed.

Rosh Hashanah (Jewish New Year) and Yom Kippur (The Day of Atonement) challenged Mark again to cover every voice part with the required number of singers. He would sometimes have to phone employers to ask permission for those who were not Jewish to attend, and also to include an overflow choir. For the High Holy Days, the synagogue was packed. Some of the music was truly moving, the combination of singing and fasting an unforgettable, marathon experience.

After the departure of Rabbi Reinhart to the Westminster Synagogue, Rabbi Van Der Zyl was appointed as senior minister of the West London Synagogue in 1958. Probably the most beloved rabbi in Britain, amongst both Jews and Gentiles, was Rabbi Hugo Gryn who served as assistant minister from 1964-68. A survivor of Auschwitz, he had received his rabbinic training in the United States, but spent his professional life in England and became a leading voice in the field of Interfaith. He also participated in the BBC Radio 4's 'The Moral Maze,' and was an advisor on religious broadcasting. From 1968 he became the senior rabbi at the WLS where he remained until his death in 1996. 5.

Sir Winston Churchill finally died, aged ninety, following a stroke, on 24th January 1965. He was held in such admiration and gratitude by royalty, government and people that he was honoured with a state funeral which took place at St Paul's Cathedral on 30th January. For a number of days before that, hundreds of thousands of mourners filed past his lying in state at Westminster Hall, waiting patiently in wind and rain to pay their respects to the inspirational figure who had guided the country and Commonwealth through the darkest days of the war, from seeming hopelessness to eventual victory over Nazism. The cost had been great.

Tributes to the unparalleled leadership of Sir Winston which led to the destruction of Nazism and the preservation of the free world were paid by Anglo-Jewish congregations; the Federation of Synagogues, Reform and Liberal. In London, memorial services were held in his honour at the West London Synagogue, Bevis Marks and at the Liberal Synagogue in St. John's Wood. 6.

At the West London Synagogue, the memorial service was unforgettable in its heartfelt poignancy. The large, august building was crammed on the ground floor and in the gallery with loyal Jewish Londoners, all wanting to pay their respects; there was not a spare seat, with standing room only for many. The atmosphere was electric; Mark had rehearsed and conducted specially selected music, and the whole choir sang with heart and soul. Perhaps many in the congregation had lost relatives in the Holocaust, or in the bombing of London, or were on active service during the war, the horror of those times never to be erased from their memories even though life had to go on.

The contribution from the two rabbis who led the service was very moving, and everyone listened in silence; Rabbi Van Der Zyl who had narrowly escaped the Nazis in 1939, and Rabbi Hugo Gryn, who survived Auschwitz, although his brother and father did not. Rabbi Gryn pointed out that had it not been for Churchill's leadership and the valour of the Battle of Britain pilots in 1940, this country would have been invaded. The general population would have been subjugated by Nazism, but the Jews would have been annihilated.

The Israeli government proposed to complete the campaign for the Winston Churchill Forest in Lower Galilee, near the city of Nazareth, on the 100th anniversary of the late Prime Minister's birth, 1974, and to inform Lady Churchill accordingly. "The project will establish a living memorial to the man who will be remembered in history as our faithful friend, and the champion of freedom."At least 300,000 trees were needed, and at present the forest consists of mostly pine and eucalyptus trees. 7.

By 1964, Roger, Mark's son, was appointed to the staff of the Winterthur Conservatoire in Switzerland where he taught violin and chamber-music on a full-time basis until 1968 when he returned to Britain, although he continued to give regular master classes in Winterthur. He also had the honour of being invited to lead the Zurich Chamber Orchestra, but turned it down due to the frequent amount of travel it would have involved, causing absence from his family. He also gave a series of short, intensive courses for advanced students and professionals at Dartington Hall in Devon, just as his father had done more than twenty years earlier. 8.

Sadly for Mark and Eva, Jane and her artist husband, Laszlo Szilvassy, decided to emigrate to Canada with their two daughters, Alexandra and Nadia in 1967. It was an emotional wrench for them all, but particularly for Eva who had lost most of her Polish relatives, and would now no longer see her daughter, son-in-law and granddaughters on a regular basis. It was as if history was repeating itself, since on her marriage, Eva had left her parents and family in Palestine in 1926 to start a new life in England. She wrote to them in Canada unfailingly every week, and they visited London twice or more each year.

In 1968, Mark, as old as the century, retired from his appointment as director of music of the West London Synagogue after over 30 years of service. His place was filled by Sydney Fixman, and Arnold Richardson continued as organist until his death in 1972.

In the synagogue review of January 1968, Rabbi Jonathan Magonet pays tribute to Mark's long service in an article entitled, **'If Music Be the Food of Prayer'**. The script follows:

"West London has always seemed the epitome of conservatism; a solid Victorian institution where nothing ever changes –at the same time it has taken the lead in ideas and innovations any number of times in the history of the Reform movement. This paradox is very obvious in the history of Mr Mark Raphael, the choirmaster, who is retiring now after thirty-one years in the post.

Over coffee he talked in his enthusiastic, sprightly way about the music that has been his whole life. Born at the turn of the century in the East End, by the age of ten he was already a synagogue chorister, being 'elevated' soon to the Great Synagogue, Duke's Place, Aldgate. Here for three years, under the famous choirmaster Samuel Alman, he was the alto soloist. Here also he heard some of the greatest cantors of the time, including Cantor Katz who had a great influence on him. He speaks affectionately of the 'fat, sweet, languorous man with an exquisite, lyrical voice' whose relaxed singing he learned.

Educated at Jews' Free School, he left home at fourteen for a brief career in the Music Hall, sharing the bill with stars such as

Marie Lloyd, as a member of 'Carrie Laurie's Juveniles,' where his speciality was an imitation of Caruso. Difficult years came when his voice began to break, but his musical career began in earnest with a scholarship to the Royal Academy of Music. His training extended to periods in Paris, Milan and Berlin, and gradually he gained a growing international reputation as a concert and lieder singer. He met his Polish wife, Eva, in Vienna and married her during a visit to Palestine in 1926, when he also met her parents.

His association with West London began in 1933 when the choirmaster asked him to lead the overflow service. His own setting of *Hashivenu* got him his present post when it fell vacant in 1936, working with the organist Dr Percy Rideout who encouraged (and firmly criticized) his compositions.

'The thing I have loved best has been composing – it makes me very happy when, if one of my pieces is omitted, a member of the congregation asks, "Why don't you stick to the traditional music?! " It's very pleasing to know they have become part of the life of the Synagogue.'

Innovations of any sort have always been hotly debated at West London. Once when he introduced his own version of *Lechah Dodi* he found a great discussion going on following the service. A woman told him: "Oh, Mr Raphael, you're a great choirmaster, and you have a lovely voice – but as a composer, you're *lousy*!" Needless to say the tune is now the standard West London version.

One irate member, after he had introduced a traditional version of *Adon Olam,* burst out: "Mr Raphael, I can see you changing the tune of 'God Save the Queen'!"

One of the criticisms levelled against the service is the lack of congregational participation, and it has always been his concern to set the 'popular' songs in a singable form. He even began some years ago an evening teaching session for members of the congregation who wished to learn the melodies, but this petered out through lack of support.

Though retiring from West London, Mr Raphael continues to be active as Professor of Singing at the Royal College of Music. His influence will continue to be felt with affection and gratitude as long as his beautiful music continues to adorn the Berkeley Street Service."

Mark was still busy teaching singing at the Royal College of Music, and equally so with private tuition at 17 St. John's Wood Terrace. His career as a concert singer, and soloist/conductor at the West London Synagogue had come to an end, but he continued to use his voice, and to impart his love of singing and passion for music to others, providing them with sage advice and the wealth of his own rich experience. He also continued to support his college students with great enthusiasm at many of their evening concerts, whether for oratorio, opera or recitals.

Throughout the sixties, despite his heavy workload, Mark also composed a good deal. He wrote an enchanting song, dedicated to his granddaughters, entitled 'The Fly,' set to a poem by William Blake, published in 1961 by Elkin &Co. Published at the same time was 'To Electra,' set to a romantic poem by Robert Herrick (1591-1674). Also published in 1961 to words by William Shakespeare was 'Shall I compare thee to a summer's day?' dedicated to Nancy Carne. In 1963, Elkin also published, 'The Shepherd' set to a poem by William Blake, and dedicated to Nora Forman, Jane's godmother. Most touchingly in 1963, Mark dedicated to his wife, Eva, a song set to John Fletcher's (1579-1625) poem, 'Weep No More'. Eva had by now lost her one surviving sister, Rushzka, in Israel, from lung cancer.

Weep no more, nor sigh nor groan,
Sorrow calls no time that's gone:
Violets plucked, the sweetest rain
Makes not fresh nor grow again,

Trim thy locks, look cheerfully,
Fate's hid ends eyes cannot see,
Joys as winged dreams fly fast
Why should sadness longer last?
Grief is but a wound to woe;
Gentlest fair, mourn, mourn no more.

1. Information from Mrs Irene Raphael
2. Information from Mrs Jane Szilvassy
3. Description of the West London Synagogue Wikipedia
4. Jessica Wyman. Jewish Gen
5. West London Synagogue Archives at Southampton University
6. The Jewish Chronicle, January 1965
7. The Winston Churchill Forest in Israel Wikipedia
8. Information from Mrs Irene Raphael

Mark teaching at the Royal College of Music

Eva in her garden in St John's Wood

Chapter 13

The Final Years

During his early seventies, Mark enjoyed an Indian summer of energy and musical fulfilment, despite the conclusion both of his recital days and of his involvement at the West London Synagogue. His teaching at the Royal College of Music continued undiminished, as did the private tuition. One student, Chris Gulley, who studied with Mark at the Royal College in 1972 and 1973, remembers him and his guidance with great respect and affection; the songs of Roger Quilter are particularly memorable to him. Chris became a well-known bass-baritone recitalist, and additionally, a song man at York Minster. As a teacher of singing, among many others, he is now passing on Mark's experience and knowledge to his own pupils.

Throughout the decade, Mark's love of composition continued with the setting of three D H Lawrence love poems: 'Dog-tired,' 'Cherry Robbers' and 'Flapper,' for high voice and piano, published by Thames Publishing in 1973. The three Blake Songs: 'The Shepherd,' 'The Fly' and 'The Lamb' for medium voice and piano, were republished by Roberton Publications of Wendover in 1976. Two songs set to poems by Thomas Moore (1779-1852) for solo voice and piano:' When through the Piazzetta,' and 'At the Mid-hour of Night,' were also published by Roberton in 1978. Some of Mark's songs were later used for the Associated Board Singing Examinations. 1.

The harmonious rhythm of his life with Eva continued, notwithstanding occasional bouts of illness. During the holidays from his teaching at the Royal College of Music, over the years, they were able to pay numerous visits to Canada to see their daughter, Jane, Laszlo, their son-in –law, and their two granddaughters, Alexandra and Nadia. Although Eva's sister, Ruszcha, had sadly died of lung cancer in the early sixties, Mark and Eva were able to travel to Israel to see her daughter, Ani, possibly other Polish relatives who had emigrated to Israel before the war and, of course, their adopted son, Joe. He married Margaret Stern in 1956 and they had three sons: Yuval, Daniel and Raphael .Having gained his D Phil at Oxford University, Joe became Associate Professor at the Hebrew University of Jerusalem. Tragically they lost their eldest son, Yuval, during his army service in 1976. 2.

In 1971, Mark and Eva were proud that their son, Roger, was appointed Senior Lecturer at the Royal Scottish Academy of Music and Drama in Edinburgh. He also taught at St Mary's Music School which he helped to found. This is a school for musically gifted children, similar to the Yehudi Menuhin School. Its vibrant choir serves St Mary's Episcopalian Cathedral. He participated at the Dartington Summer School and in the European String Teachers' Association, where his playing attracted the attention of two composers who wrote works especially for him: Three Etudes for Violin and Piano by Soulima Stravinsky, and the Sonata for Violin by Helen Glatz. Roger had developed a faultless violin technique, no matter how demanding the music, and like his father before him, had become an exceptional teacher. 3.

On 4th January, 1974, the press caught the attention of Mark and others in its report that the autographed manuscript of the original draft of the first Yiddish grand opera, 'King Ahaz,' first performed at the Yiddish Opera House in the Commercial Road in London's East End in 1912(and in which young Mark, aged 12 years, had portrayed a minor role) was currently on offer by antiquarian booksellers, Travis and Emery. 4.

The opera, of course, was composed and written by Samuel Alman, best known as a composer of liturgical music, who died in 1947. The article revealed that on 16th March, 1912, its first performance required police to control the crowds outside the theatre. Inside, the audience ate sandwiches!

In 1912, *The Star* had referred to 'an audience which, though it partook of refreshment all through the performance, was as discriminating as it was eager to be pleased.' 'Candid Critic' in *Reynolds News* commented, 'Your Jewish playgoer knows what he likes, and allows no mistaken ideas of decorum to chill his manifestation of pleasure'. The *Manchester Guardian* found the opera to be surprisingly good, and *The Star* critic wrote, "Till Saturday, Samuel Alman was unknown; now it would not be surprising if he ultimately made a considerable reputation for himself beyond the limits of the community to which he belongs."

What brought Samuel Alman's niece, Dr Gertrude Hardie, to take the manuscript to Travis and Emery was her difficulty in disposing of her uncle's effects. This was probably following the death of Alman's widow. She approached various Jewish societies after her uncle died, but they were not interested in the manuscripts of his music. The Jewish Memorial Council took the synagogue music, and various choirs took the sheet music, but a great deal remained, and she could not store it. The story had a happy ending though, since the complete manuscript of Melech Ahaz (King Ahaz) is now in the library of the Hebrew University in Jerusalem; a copy is at the British Library. 5.

Mark proved to be a great champion of his old teacher, and a loyal friend. In the same year (1974), in collaboration with Gertrude Hardie, he assisted Elie Delieb in writing a biography of Samuel Alman which was published in the 1974 April/May issue of the *Cantors' Review*. In view of the composer's talent, his translation of classical operas into Yiddish for performances at the Temple of Art, and his life-long devotion to the propagation of Jewish music, Mark had a few straight comments to make. He considered Alman's Lieder to be as great as those of Hugo Wolf and Franz Schubert. He explained that many years before, in 1929, he had given a concert of Alman's Lieder at the Wigmore Hall; the non-Jewish critics raved about the music, but the Jewish public did not understand it at all, and he heard a lot of adverse comments. Then, a few years later, Mark tried to form an Alman Society to record his works, but nothing came of it. He recalled that in days gone by, Jews in the East End lived in dire poverty, and people like Alman 'made life lovely for them. Today, they're only interested in cars!'

Sadly, Kitty, half-sister to both Jack and Mark, died in 1974, as did Nora Forman, Jane's godmother, who had done so much to help the family in the early years. Jane de Glehn, another great friend of the family, died in 1977. In July 1975, Mark gave his last singing lesson at the Royal College of Music, and retired, though his bevy of private pupils still regularly frequented the music room of 17 St John's Wood Terrace. His drive for composition also continued.

At this time, several London cantors who had previously studied or were still studying at Jews' College, came to Mark for voice lessons. Michael Isdale, baritone, who is currently the cantor at the South Manchester Orthodox Synagogue, now located in Bowdon, Greater Manchester, studied with Mark privately for a year in 1974 and recalled the structure of the lessons, and the Vaccai exercises which so many singers value. 6. Chazan Dov Speier took lessons with Mark in 1974 and 1975 whilst he was in London, but was also trained in Sweden (where he was born), Belgium and Israel. He recalls Mark's advice about the need for the singer to be very relaxed, with a dropped jaw and no tension. Knowing that she was to visit Israel, Eva took lessons in Hebrew with Rev Speier, and unsurprisingly, as a true linguist, she made great progress. Rev Speier currently serves as a freelance cantor both in the UK and abroad. He is also considered as a concert chazan, and gives operatic recitals. 7.

Chazan Steve Robins, a tenor whose voice resembled that of Tito Schipa, studied with Mark for about eight years from 1972 onwards, gaining his ARCM (Associate of the Royal College of Music) with him whilst taking lessons privately every week. He would sing a diverse collection of pieces, ranging from opera to Lieder to Mark's own songs. Currently chazan at the Woodside Park Synagogue in London, at the age of 68, with no noticeable change in his voice, Rev Robins attributes his vocal longevity to Mark Raphael's brilliant teaching. He also realised, as did others, that Mark would have preferred to be a tenor himself, rather than a baritone. Interestingly, in the late seventies, he began to sing in the tenor range. 8

Chazan Johnny Gluck, a tenor with a glorious voice and an obvious ease of singing, studied with Mark, and pursued his musical education at the Royal College of Music whilst serving as chazan with the Marble Arch congregation from 1970 to 1975. In 1975, he went to Israel, and later to South Africa. Tragically he died in 1984, at the age of 36. (His voice can be heard on Youtube) 9.

Another highly gifted chazan, Meir Finkelstein, was born in Israel in 1951, but moved to England with his family in 1955. He studied with Mark in the seventies, graduating from the Royal College of Music with an ARCM in voice, composition and piano whilst serving as chazan at the Golders Green Synagogue. He later moved to America where in addition to serving in prestigious synagogues in Illinois and California, he enjoyed a successful career as a prolific composer/arranger and lecturer. 10.

Mark's star pupil, in terms of cantors, was undoubtedly Naftali Herstik, whose family emigrated from Hungary to Israel when he was three. Descended from a long line of cantors and rabbis, he was soon recognized as a child prodigy. Whilst serving as chazan at the Finchley Synagogue for seven years from 1972, he completed his education at the Royal College of Music, studying voice with Mark . Whilst in London, he gave a recital at the Wigmore Hall, which was a huge success and which both Mark and Eva attended. He returned to Israel, and became the chief cantor of the Great Synagogue in Jerusalem. His wonderful tenor voice would soar up effortlessly in expression of Hebrew prayers, and was truly moving. Unsurprisingly, he has had a worldwide reputation as a superb concert artist, and more recently as the director of the Tel Aviv Cantorial Institute. 11.

BBC Radio 3 marked the 100th anniversary of Roger Quilter's birth in November 1977 with three mornings devoted to recitals of his songs. On the first morning Mark Raphael was invited to talk about Quilter and his singers, and with material from the BBC's archives, he introduced some of the recordings he made with the composer, as well as recordings made by Gervase Elwes and Roland Hayes.7.A transcript of Mark's contribution to the programme follows:

Mark Raphael:

I first met Roger Quilter in 1923. I had given a Wigmore Hall recital which included his 'Three Blake Songs,' and Quilter was in the audience. After the recital, he came round to the artists' room, and was most appreciative of my singing of his songs. A few days later, he asked me to call and see him at his home in Montagu Street, and there on the piano was a new song he'd written specially for me. 'The Jealous Lover', was one of a set dedicated to me, called Jacobean Lyrics. From this time on, a friendship and professional partnership grew, which was to last right up to his death in 1953.When he was young, his hair was fair. He was very tall and thin, his eyes were almost sea green, his face as if it had been carved from stone. When in company and somewhat worried, he stammered. I rarely saw him frown, though I have seen him writhe in acute pain. He was very shy and never recovered completely from an illness in his early thirties. In repose, he seemed to be gently smiling. He was one of the kindest persons I have ever known, and he was happiest when in some practical or material way, he was able to help someone less fortunate than himself.

With people of his own affluent class, he felt really at home only when they loved the arts. This was specially the case with Mr And Mrs De Glehn. Wilfrid de Glehn was an RA and many first performances of Quilter's songs were heard in de Glehn's studio in Chelsea. I remember on one occasion when I introduced 'The Fuchsia Tree,' Pablo Casals and Sargent the painter were there. Wilfrid de Glehn's portrait of Quilter now hangs in the National Portrait Gallery. For Quilter, composition was a slow, painstaking and fastidious process, and he envied the facility of Cyril Scott, and the originality of Percy Grainger who had been his fellow students at the Frankfurt Conservatoire. Quilter often said that he loved lyrical poetry more than music, and so often his setting of words creates for the singer the problem of having to decide, whether to phrase and breathe according to the words or music. His overriding passion was for flowers and trees, and many of his songs have flower titles:'Now sleeps the Crimson Petal', 'Go Lovely Rose,' 'The Fuchsia Tree'.

The first English song I ever sang was his setting of Herrick's 'To Daisies'.

(A recording follows of Mark Raphael singing 'To Daisies')

Before the 1st World War, the tenor Gervase Elwes was among many singers who sang Quilter's songs, and I think he gave the first performance of the 'Three Shakespeare Songs'. Quilter often spoke about Elwes's singing, who was at his best in oratorio, especially as the Evangelist in Bach's St. Matthew Passion, and in Elgar's 'Dream of Gerontius'. Most of all, Quilter admired his diction and feeling for words as well as his musical phrasing. Here is Gervase Elwes singing 'Fair House of Joy' and 'Fill a Glass with Golden Wine.'

(A recording follows of Gervase Elwes singing 'Fair House of Joy', and 'Fill a Glass with Golden Wine)

Gervase Elwes who came from a wealthy Catholic family, was killed when he fell beneath a moving train while on a concert tour in North America in 1921. As a memorial to him, his teacher, Victor Beigel, Roger Quilter and other leading musicians, started a Gervase Elwes Memorial Fund, later to become the Musicians' Benevolent Fund. Here's another recording by Elwes, 'Love's Philosophy', dedicated to him. This is one of the more robust songs, and its rousing climax has always been popular with singers and audiences alike.

(A recording follows of Elwes singing 'Love's Philosophy')

Another singer Quilter admired was the black American tenor, Roland Hayes, who made his London debut in 1920. He made several highly successful visits to Europe, in the 20s, and after a warmly received Wigmore Hall recital in 1921, sang at Buckingham Palace to King George V and Queen Mary. Here he is singing Quilter's 'It was a Lover and His Lass'.

(A recording follows of Roland Hayes singing 'It was a Lover and His Lass'.

The Roland Hayes singing aroused the interest of Dame Nellie Melba, who also sang Quilter's songs, in fact the 'Cuckoo' is dedicated to her. I think it says a great deal for the quality of Quilter's songs, that they should have attracted the interest of singers of such different backgrounds and temperaments. Mind you, I was born here in London, my parents came from Poland. Quilter used to say that my lieder approach to his songs appealed very much to him. In the 30s, Schott's published a number of his songs with German translations. I sang them in Germany and Austria, where reviewers picked out 'Come Away Death'- 'Komm'Herbei Tod', and 'Weep you no more, sad fountains'—'Weih' nicht mehr, traurige Queller', and placed them in the lieder class.

(A recording follows of Mark Raphael singing 'Weep you no more sad Fountains'.

I must say that I have always loved singing and teaching Quilter's songs, and I often think of our relationship as friends and artists, and the numerous concerts we gave together, and of the deep concern the mental illness of his last years gave to me, my wife and his closest friends.

As time passes, it becomes clearer to me that the songs and the man are one...kind, gracious, a lyrical being, desiring to please. 12.

(A recording follows of Mark Raphael singing 'Go Lovely Rose'.)

A song recital by Mark Raphael, baritone, originally recorded by Columbia (England), was re-issued in 1985 by Musique Internationale of Chicago. The recording features two English composers: Samuel Alman and Roger Quilter. The record was reviewed in *Musica Judaica* (1985/86 Vol.8) by Marko Rothmüller. Mark Raphael was closely associated with both composers.

Rothmüller writes: "Mark Raphael is remembered as a concertizing artist, and also as an outstanding voice teacher and vocal coach...

The four Alman songs are recognizably rooted in the melodic arsenal of East-European cantillation. They combine the old modes (Phrygian, for instance) with major and minor keys, including the augmented 2nd interval. Alman's songs are very well written for the voice, with colourful accompaniments. Raphael sings them beautifully with astounding East-European expression, although he was born in London, and lived there all his life. These songs, also by the manner in which they are sung, have a distinct religious mood and flavour.

Quite different are the songs by Roger Quilter (1877-1953) with whom Raphael was in personal contact. Quilter received his main musical training in Germany, and he is well known for a variety of musical compositions, especially his songs and his splendid arrangements of old English songs. Characteristically, as far as the musical style is concerned, treatment of the piano accompaniment and writing for the voice...for the songs on this recording...Alman and Quilter are quite similar, although the latter allows the singer greater opportunity for a variety of expression.

This brings us again to Mark Raphael whose beautiful and gentle, lyrical baritone voice is quite flexible in all registers, and who sings all these songs with warm feeling. His technical abilities are remarkable, particularly in the high range, where he is able to express great tenderness and gentleness. His diction is excellent, which contributes to the fact that the recording is a thoroughly enjoyable recital."

The late Barry Serota wrote the notes on the record cover which included much information about Quilter, Alman and Mark Raphael himself. In the penultimate paragraph he writes: 'Beyond his career as a vocal performer, Mr Raphael has distinguished himself as one of London's leading vocal coaches, and in this capacity he has worked with some of the leading singers of the world, including Marian Anderson and Gigli. He has also had a rich career as a synagogue choral conductor and composer.'

In the final paragraph he writes: 'Musique Internationale expresses kind thanks to Mark Raphael for his efforts in facilitating this re-issue. Thanks are also due to Mr David Hall of the New York Public Library's Rodgers and Hammerstein Collection for securing tape transcriptions of the Quilter recordings, and Professor Eli Segal, for transcribing the Alman discs which Mr Raphael so graciously brought to the United States on a visit in the fall of 1981'.

Persistent hoarseness and some loss of singing voice in the late seventies, lead Mark to consult an Ear, Nose and Throat specialist at St. Mary's Hospital, Paddington. Following a biopsy, cancer of the larynx was diagnosed, a condition not wholly uncommon in male professional singers aged over 60 who have smoked. If treated in its early stages with radiotherapy, there is a good chance of cure. The treatment often involves short, daily doses with a rest at weekends, and can last between three to seven weeks. Mark made an excellent recovery, and claimed he could sing better than well before the cancer was diagnosed. Judging from a recording dated around 1980, his voice is in remarkably good condition, with an improved upper register.

He had triumphed over cancer, and, predictably, he returned to his teaching, singing and writing. In 1981, Roberton (Wendover) published two of his songs: 'Row gently here', and 'Oh! Breathe not his name'; both songs were for solo voice and piano, the words written by Thomas Moore (1779 -1852).

A new star pupil, Mark Glanville, bass-baritone, a graduate of Oxford University and a writer, took voice lessons with Mark for several years, from the end of the seventies, which he still values to this day. On meeting Raphael for the first time, he described him as impish and radiant, yet possessing the presence and authority of someone a foot taller. It was specifically for Mark Glanville that Mark Raphael, aged over eighty, recorded two CDs of his repertoire: works ranging from' Arie Antiche', to Schubert and Schumann, Brahms, Tosti, Fauré, Duparc, Wolf, Quilter and some of his own songs. Amazingly, he accompanied himself on the piano and announced each piece.

There have been, without doubt, more remarkable voices than Mark Raphael's, but his musicality, his impeccable diction, vocal technique and above all his gift of getting to the heart of each song, enabled him to communicate its message with great beauty, as if he were personally experiencing that emotion, in a way that many greater voices could not. A quarter of a century later, his interpretation of these songs still have the power to touch the heart; that is the test of the artist.

Mark Glanville later won a scholarship to continue his studies at the Royal Northern College of Music. He forged an operatic career for himself, singing at Opera North, Scottish Opera,

Lisbon Opera and New Israeli Opera, as well as making regular recordings. In recent years, his work moved from the opera house to the recital hall with the song cycle 'Yiddish Winterreise' – A Holocaust Survivor's Inner Journey told through Yiddish song. Using traditional Yiddish folk songs, many arranged by the composer/accompanist, Dr Alexander Knapp, Mark Glanville took Schubert's 'Winterreise' "as a symbol for the destruction of home and family," and together, they accomplished a successful tour in the United States during the spring of 2011.

Sadly, Israel Wiseblatt, Mark's half brother, and his junior by about ten years, known throughout his life as Pip, died in 1981.

As fate would have it, when Mark (Raphael) went into St Mary's Paddington for routine prostate surgery in the mid eighties, he sustained a serious stroke during the operation, and lost some of the feeling on the right side of his body. During this time, Eva was far from well, and eventually colon cancer was diagnosed. Mark's nephew, Raymond, and his wife, Pat, living locally in St. John's Wood, were able to be a great help to them both. For her part, Jane flew over from Canada several times to care for her parents.

Eva was admitted to St. Mary's Hospital, and was subsequently transferred to Hereford Lodge in Paddington where she died of a pulmonary embolism on 17th March 1984. Thus ended a life of devotion to her husband and family. The funeral took place at Golders Green Crematorium; her ashes were scattered in the rose garden.

Despite his physical handicaps, Mark, always positive and ready for a challenge, confronted life's problems head on, and taught himself to play the piano with his left hand. He was even able to give some lessons, and play excerpts from 'King Ahaz.' Yet, after a long, harmonious marriage to Eva, he did not adapt to single life well. As a stroke victim, the practicalities of looking after himself became all too much, so with the family's support, he chose to leave St John's Wood to take up residence at Dulas

Court in Hereford, one of the Musicians' Benevolent Homes, where he hoped to live with like-minded people.

It was touching for his visiting relatives, who had come at various times from London, Scotland, Canada and Somerset, to see him immersed in setting one of William Blake's poems to music, regardless of his stroke, and with only his left hand operational. Music was almost everything to him. On one occasion, he somehow organised a flight from Bristol to visit his son, Roger and family who were living in Scotland. His joy to be with them, combined with the beauty of the scenery, caused him to emit a very loud, high, sustained note, proving that his voice was still functioning!

As time passed, despite the good care at Dulas Court, Mark was not altogether happy in Hereford. It may have been due to his deteriorating health being no longer adequately supported by a residential home, or a clash of personalities, or the distance from London resulting in fewer visitors for him. Whatever the reason, he was moved to Little Hayes Nursing Home, Kenley, near Croydon. On 1st February 1988, he died there of cerebral thrombosis, with Roger, and his adopted son, Joe, at his bedside.

Assimilated into non-Jewish society and agnostic, yet totally loyal to his Jewish roots, and unashamed of his childhood poverty in the East End as a Yiddisher Cockney, Mark's irrepressible love of life, music and culture, his humour and humanity, were no more. His funeral was held at the Golders Green Crematorium, and his ashes scattered in the rose garden.

A poignant memorial service was held for him on 5th September, 1988, at the West London Synagogue, when some of his religious music was sung by the choir, and conducted by Sydney Fixman, the director of music. Relatives, friends, colleagues and pupils, Jews and Gentiles, many of them in tears, paid their respects and said their final goodbyes. All present knew his worth, and some appreciated his endearing inclusiveness to Christians as well as Jews; they would not see his like again. He had touched their lives and they would not forget him. His legacy would live on in his pupils, his compositions and recordings, and in the memories of those who loved him.

1. Information from the Royal College of Music
2. Information from Dr Danny Taglicht and Mrs Margaret Taglicht
3. Information from Mrs Irene Raphael
4. Jewish Chronicle, January 1974.
5. Jewish Chronicle, January 1974
6. Information from Chazan Michael Isdale
7. Information from Chazan Dov Speier
8. Information from Chazan Steve Robins
9. Chazan Johnny Gluck Wikipedia
10. Chazan Meier Finkelstein Wikipedia
11. Information from Steve Robins and Wikipedia
12. BBC's Radio 3 broadcast in November 1977 on 'Quilter and His Singers' to mark the 100th anniversary of Quilter's birth...

Roger, Mark and Joe in London ,1975

Joe Taglicht with his family in Israel, 1975. From left to right-Joe, Danny, Yuval and Margaret. Rafi the youngest is in front.

Mark, aged 84 at 17 St John's Wood Terrace

Mark in his eighties , at 17 St John's Wood Terrace

Singing and The Art of Breathing

by
Mark Raphael

Among the many letters which Caruso wrote to his wife, there was one which gave me much food for thought. Within two weeks, he was to sing Rodolfo in Puccini's 'La Boheme'. He wrote that the days previous to singing that part, he breathed Rodolfo. He felt he was breathing lyrically. Before singing Radames from Aida, the dramatic and lyrical tensions of this part affected him quite differently. He breathed and lived Radames.

There is no doubt that any other highly sensitive singer would feel the same, but I have never read or heard it stated so revealingly.

The extreme sensitivity of our respiratory organs is a scientific fact. I once read an article on this subject in which two men were looking at the colour, red. The subtly different reactions of their respiratory organs were recorded on a screen. Other demonstrations prove beyond dispute that our feelings, thoughts, health, movements, and the very things we gaze upon, fundamentally affect our breathing.

Although it is obvious that no two people are alike, theoretically we are all made of the same stuff. But to teach breathing from a purely theoretical angle, I consider both wrong and harmful. Wrong, because this approach is far removed from that required by the sensitive art of singing, harmful, because it so often defeats its aims.

How often singers come to me for tuition, having worked on a method of breath control, who had neither control not art. Years spent in trying to master a theory of breathing have robbed them of spontaneity and poise.

Breathing for us singers should be a deeply seated subtle and sensitive function. It should always be identified musically with the work in hand, be it exercise, vocalise or song.

There is nothing to stop one from learning how the respiratory organs function in relation to the vocal chords. This knowledge can best be acquired from scientists. When a book is written by a scientist in collaboration with a singing-teacher, it can be most useful to us. Such a book I consider "The Mechanics of Singing" by Evetts and Worthington (published by Dent) in which we learn of a mechanism that no man-made can equal; we learn too how in diverse ways man disrupts it.

There may be many singers who haven't either the patience or aptitude for acquiring a scientific knowledge of how the vocal apparatus works. But there is no excuse for knowing nothing at all of the theory of music. A feeling of insecurity, caused by not being able to sight-read and sing in time, is so often responsible for thwarting spontaneous expression.

This kind of insecurity shows itself mainly in tightness of the jaw, inflexibility of the tongue, anxiety to reach high notes and singing out of tune. In this condition sensitive co-operation between the breathing and the voice is impossible.

When you think how simple it is to acquire a moderate standard of sight-reading, you wonder why it is that so many singers are such incredibly bad musicians.

Breathing exercises to strengthen the respiratory muscles may well achieve their limited aim, but I am convinced that continual expressive use of the voice, without undue stress and strain, not only strengthens the muscles, but increases their sensitivity, which should, after all, be the aim of every serious singer.

In the early stages, exercises should be simple and musical. Vocalises are useful, providing the development is by easy stages. The 'Vaccai' Vocalises are I think the best of this kind. All vocal requirements, such as legato, agility, skips and embellishments etc. are here most musically presented. In this early stage there is no reason why a song or aria should not be included, providing it is not too elaborate in texture.

Whatever the work in hand, be it song, vocalise or exercise, the shape, length, range, rise and fall of the phrase should be <u>musically</u> anticipated. The respiratory organs will respond to this approach will respond to this approach far more directly than they would to a merely mechanical taking of breath.

Why is it that some singers with big voices have no feeling or imagination? Everything they sing sounds the same. All that has been demanded of their respiratory muscles is to support one kind of strident tone. They even take pride in demonstrating the strength of their diaphragm. On the other hand there are singers who cultivate a kind of refined crooning. Both the loud bellowing type and the refined precious singer have developed one kind of breathing suitable to their way of singing. Any attempt on the part of the shouter to sing softly ends in disaster; the refined crooner's attempt to crescendo results in hollow hooting. Breathing has ceased to be an art. The forceful singer develops either a tremolo or a slow vibrato. Continual without variation becomes dull and often breathy. It also develops into the so-called microphone singing, devoid of tension and life.

The usual kind of breath control often leads to holding back. The tone cannot flow freely, and progression and variation are difficult.

Working continually at florid exercises can be harmful if the aim, in singer's parlance, is just to warm up the voice.

A flexible, variable, free, smooth tone can best be acquired through a musical approach. Among the many legato arias for women's voices you have only to think of Purcell's "When I am laid in Earth", and Bellini's "Ah! non credea" to realise the difference in mood and style. Sensitive awareness is essential for developing an art of breathing. The respiratory system should be trained to respond and support the voice, to heighten and lessen only through the varying musical approach. Not only is the breath the source of life, the respiratory system is for the serious singer the foundation of his art.

It is obvious that the partnership between breathing and singing would be imperfect without the harmonious cooperation of the respiratory muscles, the vocal chords and the resonating cavities. It is possible, step by step, to bring this to partnership to perfection, from simple exercises, vocalises and songs to elaborate compositions and arias.

The mechanics of learning a piece of music, rhythm, time values, notes and words etc. should be mastered first. If only singers would develop a keen sense of inner hearing. The advantages are enormous. You can acquire a habit of learning your music without giving physical utterance. It requires little breath to bring to life what you in your inner ear have heard. What has been perhaps a pale reflection comes to life as a sensitive reality. You have learnt your music without the worry of range, mastered rhythm and time values, memorised your words; the complete work now slumbers as it were in your inner ear. You are now ready to bring the music to life. The respiratory muscles are free to respond to expressive singing.

One cannot imagine any one singer being capable of every style of music, but within the limits of a singer's gifts and capabilities, great and subtle variety is possible. Take, for example, the part of Gilda in Verdi's Rigoletto, usually sung by a coloratura soprano. The staccato and legato passages Verdi gives her to sing in the famous 'Caro Nome' aria, the duets with her father and the Duke, her part in the famous quintet, are all subtly different. To re-create Verdi's creation, technique alone and just knowing where to take a breath will not help. The respiratory organs should be used as a foundation for expressive singing, for interpretation, not just to take breath, or support a <u>uniform</u> kind of staccato, florid and legato singing.

When we sing we <u>do</u> get a sensation of resonance in the mask, mouth, pharynx, nose, chest or head, according to the pitch of the note we are singing. The sensations are caused by the varying shapes of the mobile parts of the vocal apparatus, such as mouth, pharynx and the soft palate, which are occasioned by variations in pitch. These shapes in themselves are only the effect of a deeper cause, that is to say, the impulse to produce a particular pitch. This impulse, providing there is no artificial interference, will of itself result in the appropriate shaping, whereas any approach to the problem from the other end, that is to say a mechanical attempt at the reproduction of a particular shaping can only result in a breaking down of the instinctive co-ordination between the breathing and the voice. The respiratory muscles can either respond or be thwarted. Respond if your approach is sensitive to each shape and turn of phrase, rise and fall of tension and change of nuance, be thwarted if your approach and continuation be a purely mechanical one.

Highly sensitive singers, alive to the emotional qualities of the songs and roles they are singing have no truck with methods of high or low breathing. Like so many so-called born singers, they survive in spite of the different methods of voice production they happen to practise. Some remain completely ignorant of scientific methods. The classical example was Madame Patti. In Norman Klein's book on the life of the famous soprano, he writes of a talk she had with Jean de Resske after he had given a lesson to a soprano. She was then an old lady, he a famous singing teacher. "Tell me, Jean," she said, "what <u>is</u> this diaphragm breathing you keep talking about?"

And so I go back to where I began. Caruso consciously thought that his breathing was responding sympathetically to the different roles he was singing. However, even he was known to demonstrate how he breathed, how long he could sustain notes, how perfectly he could control the tidal movements of respiration. As I said earlier on, breathing exercises to control and strengthen the respiratory muscles may achieve their limited aim. This is not difficult. But Caruso's remarks on his breathing in regard to the roles he was singing, perhaps casually made, but most illuminating, have much more in common with <u>Art.</u>

Is it wrong to suggest that, being a born singer, it was natural for him to sing as a bird to fly? That his spontaneous approach to singing was responsible for the strength of his respiratory muscles ?

Can't we trace the same pattern in all born singers? Haven't you heard children sing loud, sustained phrases without any sense of strain? I am sure that although they have not yet received the benefit of special breathing exercises their respiratory organs are fully equal to the demands made upon them. They grow up, still singing for the sheer joy of it, and finally they take singing lessons, and are told their breathing apparatus needs special treatment. They are taught how to control the tidal movements of respiration, how to put on and release pressure. For many born singers this is the end. Their wings have been clipped.

Catalogue of Works (Secular)

Three Blake Songs: The Shepherd; The Fly; The Lamb...For medium voice and piano. Roberton Publications: Wendover, (1976)

Three D.H. Lawrence Love poems: Dog-tired; Cherry Robbers; Flapper...For high voice and piano. Thames Publishing: London (1973)

Gay Robin is seen no more. Two part song...poem by Robert Bridges

Published by J. Curwen and Sons: London (1932)

The Lamb. Song...Poem by William Blake. Published by Augener in 1937

Lay a Garland on my Herse. Song. Words by Fletcher. Published by Augener in 1937.

Love on my Heart from Heaven fell. Song. Wordsby Robert Bridges. Published by Elkin and Co. 1936

Memory. Song. Words by W.Browne. Published by Augener in 1937.

Shall I compare thee to a Summer's Day? Song. Words by William Shakespeare. Published by Elkin &Co in 1961

The Shepherd. Song. Poem by William Blake. Published by Elkin & Co. In 1963

Sleep. Song. Poem by J.Fletcher published by J Curwen & Sons in 1931

Slow Spring. Two part Song. Poem by K.Tynan. Published by Boosey and Hawkes in 1931. Part of 'The Winthrop Rogers Edition.

Two songs. 1) To Electra (Herrick) 2) The Fly (Blake) published by Elkin & Co in 1961.

'Weep no more Song'. Poem by John Fletcher (1579-1625). Published by Elkin & Co in 1963

'To Anne.' Song. Words by William A. Younger.Published by Elkin & Co. In 1938.

Two Thomas Moore Songs, for solo voice and piano. 1) When through the Piazzetta. 2) At the Mid-hour of Night. Roberton Publications,Wendover, 1978.

'Row Gently here.' 'O Breathe not his name.' Both songs for solo voice and piano. Words by Thomas Moore (1779 -1852) published by Roberton in 1981.

Catalogue of Works (Religious)

A list of religious choral music, some with organ accompaniment, by Mark Raphael, found in the five folders of music that he edited, perhaps in the 1950s, for use in the West London Synagogue.

Mah tovu – arr. MR

Veshameru – MR

Mechalkel - Lewandowski, arr. MR

May the words – MR

Nishmat – MR

Mechalkel – Lewandowski, arr. MR

Kedusha – Lewandowski, organ accomp. MR

Av Harachamim – MR

Av Harachamim – MR

Hashivenu –MR

Hashivenu – MR

Mah Tovu – MR

Mah Tovu – MR

Mah Tovu – MR

Lecha dodi – Lewandowski, arr. MR

Bar'chu et Adonai – MR

Baruch shem kevod – MR

Mi chamocha/Adonai yimloch – MR

Bayom hahu – MR

Lecha dodi – MR

Mechal kel – MR

Adonai melech /Halleluyah – MR

Hoshanna – Ancient melody, organ accomp. MR

Seven Amens – MR

Psalm 1 – MR

Psalm 15 – MR

Psalm 23 – MR

Psalm 36 – MR

Psalm 63 – MR

Psalm 67 – MR (all Psalms in English, selected verses)

Yigdal – MR

Yigdal – MR

Kadosh and Yimloch – MR

Adon olam – MR

Thou has been the help - MR

Discography

Songs 1-17 refer to private recordings of Quilter's songs for the Roger Quilter Society, in a presentation set signed by Quilter; they were reissued on Columbia at bi-monthly intervals. The RO number refers to the private recording, the DB number to the Columbia recording.

Mark Raphael (baritone), Roger Quilter (piano

1. Love's Philosophy, Three Songs, Op.3, no.1

    Matrix CA14795-5, RO75, DB1602, recorded 13th December, 1934 at the Abbey Road Studies, Studio 2, London, UK, issued February 1936

2. Come Away, Death, Three Shakespeare Songs, Op.6, no.1

    With Frederick Grinke (violin), Max Gilbert (viola), Herbert Withers (cello). Matrix CA14797-2, RO73, DB1598, recorded 8th November, 1934 at Abbey Road Studios, Studio 2, London

3. O Mistress Mine, Three Shakespeare Songs, Op. 6, no.2

    Matrix CA 14800-2, RO74, DB1629, recorded 13th December 1934, issued April 1936

4. To Daisies, To Julia, Op.8, no.4

    Matrix CA14793-2, RO76, DB1643, recorded 6th December 1934

5. Weep You No More, Seven Elizabethan Lyrics, Op, no.1

    Matrix CA14793-2, RO76, DB1643, recorded 27th November 1934

6. Song of the Blackbird, Four Songs, Op. 14, no 4

    Matrix CA14794-4, RO76, DB1643, recorded 6th December 1934

7. Where be You Going? Six Songs, Op. 18, no.2

    Matrix CA 14803-2, RO78, DB1648, recorded 29th November, 1934

8. Cherry Valley, Three Pastoral Songs, Op.22, no.2

    With Frederick Grinke(violin), Herbert Withers (cello). Matrix CA14804-3, RO78, DB1648, recorded 29 November, 1934, issued 1st August 1936.

9. Fear No More the Heat o' the Sun, Five Shakespeare Songs, Op. 23, no. 1

    Matrix CA14799-3, RO74, DB1629, recorded 6th December 1934, issued April 1936

10. It was a Lover and His Lass, Five Shakespeare Songs, Op.23, no.3

    Matrix CA14798-4, RO73, DB 1598, recorded 6th December, 1934 at the Abbey Road Studios, Studio 2, London, UK

11. Take, O Take Those Lips Away, Five Shakespeare Songs, Op.23 no. 4

    With Frederick Grinke(violin), Max Gilbert (viola), Herbert Withers (cello). Matrix CA14800-4, RO74, DB1629, recorded 13th December 1934, issued April 1936.

12. Go Lovely Rose, Five English Love Lyrics, Op.24 no. 3

    Matrix CA 14802-3, RO77, DB1583, recorded 3ed December 1934

13. O, the Month of May, Five English Love Lyrics, Op.24, no.4

    Matrix CA14801-2, RO77, DB1583, recorded 29th November 1934

14. Music, When Soft Voices Die, Six Songs, Op. 25, no.5

    Matrix CA14795-5, RO75, DB1602, recorded 13th December 1934 at Abbey Road, Studio 2, London. Issued February 1936

15. Over the Land is April, Two Songs, Op.26, no.2

    Matrix CA14803-2, RO78, DB1648, recorded 29th November 1934

16. The Jealous Lover, Five Jacobean Lyrics, Op.28, no.1

    Matrix CA14796-4, RO75, DB1602, recorded 13th December 1934, issued February 1936

17. I Dare Not Ask a Kiss, Five Jacobean Lyrics, Op. 28, no. 3

    With Frederick Grinke (violin), Max Gilbert (viola), Herbert Withers (cello). Matrix CA14796-4, RO75, DB1602, recorded 13th December 1934, issued February 1936

18. Modern Jewish Songs by Samuel Alman, with Piano. Columbia.

    Erets Aboth (Land of my Sires), and Shir Haroeth (Shepherd's Song) (4773); Al Eilah (For all these) and Lo Amuth (I shall not die) (4774) Issued 1928.

19. Songs by Wolf 1234 Columbia

    Night's Magic, Give praise to Him, and Alt, in Springtime; issued in 1934.

20. Nun wandre Maria. Herr, was trägt der Boden hier from "Spanisches Liederbuch" (Wolf).

    Gerald Moore, accompanist. HMV C3591, issued in 1947

21. Two English Composers: Samuel Alman and Roger Quilter. A Song Recital by Mark Raphael, baritone.

    Chicago: Musique Internationale M-381, originally Columbia (England) recording. Re-issued 1985/86.

22. Mark Raphael Sings. A private recording of songs selected from Mark's own repertoire for Mark Glanville…c early 80s.

Bibliography

Roger Quilter, His Life and Music by Dr Valerie Langfield

The Goldberg Variations by Mark Glanville

Children of the Ghetto by Israel Zangwill

The Jewish Immigrant in England (1870 – 1914) by Lloyd P. Gartner

Churchill and the Jews by Martin Gilbert

The Jew in London (published in 1901) by C. Russell and H.S.Lewis

The World of my Past by Abraham Biderman

The Holocaust by Martin Gilbert

Jewish London... an illustrated history by Dr Gerry Black

From Heim to Home by Nina Weiss

The International Who's Who in Music

Daniel Deronda by George Eliot

After Daybreak...the Liberation of Belsen, 1945, by Ben Shepherd

The List by Martin Fletcher

Beyond Hitler's Grasp... the heroic rescue of Bulgaria's Jews by Michael Bar-Zohar

Jewish London by Rachel Kolsky and Roslyn Rawson

Sensibility and English Song...Critical Studies of the early twentieth century by Stephen Banfield

Chasing Shadows by Rabbi Hugo Gryn and daughter Naomi Gryn

Safe Passage by Ida Cook

The Righteous by Martin Gilbert

Foley by Michael Smith

Conscience and Courage by Eva Fogelman

Grove's Dictionary of Music and Musicians

The Oxford Companion to Music by Percy Scholes

Island of Barbed Wire by Connery Chappell

Thirty Men and a Girl by Elisabeth Parry

The Lost by Daniel Mendelsohn

On Wings of Song by Wilfrid Blunt

Blooms of Darkness by Aharon Appelfeld

Brick : A Literary Journal no. 87 summer, 2011. Managing Editor: Nadia Szilvassy

Silent Rebels by Marion Schreiber

Eye Witness Auschwitz by Filip Müller

People of the Abyss by Jack Lon

LIVERPOOL LUNCH HOUR CONCERTS
for CITY WORKERS

Under the Patronage of
THE LORD MAYOR OF LIVERPOOL, Alderman Sir Sydney Jones, J.P. *and*
The Council for the Encouragement of Music and the Arts

Patrons

THIRTY-FOURTH CONCERT

CRANE THEATRE, HANOVER STREET, LIVERPOOL
(By kind permission of the Directors of Crane & Sons, Ltd.)

Wednesday, Feb. 11th, 1942, at 12.10 p.m. & 1.10 p.m.

Pianoforte and Vocal Recital *by*

MAURICE JACOBSON   MARK RAPHAEL
(Pianoforte)   *(Baritone)*

PROGRAMME

PIANOFORTE SOLO
    Romance, Op. 28, in F sharp major   ...   .   *Schumann*

SONG CYCLE
    Dichterliebe (A Poet's Love)   ...   .   *Schumann*
       'Twas in the lovely month of May ;
       From out my tears are springing ;
       The Rose and the Lily ;
       I gaze into thy tender eyes ;
       I'll breathe my soul and its yearning ;
       The Rhine, that holiest river ;
       I blame thee not ;
       If only the flowers could know it ;
       The flutes and fiddles are sounding ;
         one'er I hear them singing ;
         youth once loved a maiden ;
       Alone on a summer morning ;
       I wept as I lay dreaming ;
       At nightfall I see you ;
       The fairy-tales of childhood ;
       Old songs of tears and sorrow.

Next Concert :—WEDNESDAY, FEBRUARY 18th, 1942, at 12-10 and 1-10 p.m.
Pianoforte Recital by **CLIFFORD CURZON**

156

The Chamber Music Club.

SEASON 1924—1925.

PROGRAMME of the

Fifth Concert to be given at Lindsey Hall, The Mall,
Notting Hill Gate, W., on Tuesday Evening,
December 16th, 1924, at 8 p.m.

Trio for Pianoforte, Violin & Violoncello in G Minor
(Op. 3)   ..   .. *Chausson*

> Pas trop lent—Animé
> Vite
> Assez lent
> Animé

MRS. HERBERT WITHERS (Pianoforte)
MISS JESSIE GRIMSON (Violin)
MISS PHYLLIS HASLUCK (Violoncello)

Songs—

> " To Daisies "
> " Cherry Ripe "
> " Weep you no more "   *Roger Quilter*
> " It was lover and his lass "
> " Love's Philosophy "

MR. MARK RAPHAEL,
kindly accompanied by Mr. Roger Quilter.

INTERVAL.

Trio for Pianoforte, Violin & Horn in E♭ (Op. 40)
Brahms

> Andante
> Scherzo. Allegro
> Adagio mesto
> Finale. Allegro con brio

MRS. HERBERT WITHERS (Pianoforte)
MISS JESSIE GRIMSON (Violin)
MR. AUBREY BRAIN (Horn)

Price of Programme to Non-Members - 2/6

157

Every Evening at 8.15 o'clock

(For a limited number of weeks only)

THE BEGGAR'S OPERA

By Mr. GAY

The Music arranged and composed by
FREDERIC AUSTIN

CAST

PEACHUM......................SCOTT RUSSELL
LOCKIT....................SYDNEY GRANVILLE
MACHEATH...............FREDERICK RANALOW
FILCH .... MARK RAPHAEL
THE BEGGAR.................ARNOLD PILBEAM
MAT O' THE MINT............DEWEY GIBSON
MRS. PEACHUM.................ELSIE FRENCH
POLLY PEACHUM................ROSE HIGNELL
LUCY LOCKIT.............VIOLET MARQUESITA
DIANA TRAPES.................CICELY NICKS
JENNY DIVER...................VERA ROBSON

Drawer : DAVID HODDER   *Turnkey :* HARRY HILLIARD

Members of Macheath's Gang :
PATRICK WARD   HAROLD CHING   FRANK GOULDING
JOHN MOTTERSHEAD   CAVAN O'CONNOR

Women of the Town :
PHYLLIS DAWN   GUELDA WALLER   DORIS HALLEY-STEWART
NELLY MEYRAT   MARJORIE DIXON   MONA BENSON
BETTY WARNER   VERA MACONOCHIE

PERIOD 1728

ACT I. - - PEACHUM'S HOUSE

ACT II. Sc. i. A TAVERN. Near Newgate
       Sc. ii. NEWGATE

ACT III. Sc. i. A GAMING HOUSE
       Sc. ii. NEWGATE
       Sc. iii. THE CONDEMN'D HOLD

Produced by NIGEL PLAYFAIR

WIGMORE HALL

MARK

RAPHAEL

Song Recital

June 26th, 1929, at 8.30 p.m.

At the Piano:

GEORGE REEVES

———

BÖSENDORFER GRAND PIANOFORTE

**PROGRAMME
ONE SHILLING**

IBBS & TILLETT
124 Wigmore Street, W. 1

159

 # MUSIC in WARTIME

CONCERTS *of the* BEST MUSIC
by the BEST ARTISTS

Sponsored by The
Incorporated Society of Musicians

EVERY SUNDAY at 3.0 & 6.30

TWO CONCERTS

(SAME PROGRAMME)

Artists for Sunday November 12th :

EDA KERSEY • • *Violinist*
KATHLEEN LONG • *Pianist*
MARK RAPHAEL • • *Singer*

Violin and Piano Sonatas by Bach, Mozart and Bax ;
Songs by Schubert, Roger Quilter, &c.

THE MERCURY THEATRE

Lessees : NEW MERCURY LTD.

2 LADBROKE ROAD, NOTTING HILL GATE, W.11

1 minute Notting Hill Gate Stations.   'Buses 27, 28, 31, 46, 17, 12, 88, 32, 52.

FREE CAR PARK

◁◦◦▷

TICKETS : 5/-, 3/6 and 2/6 may be obtained from the Box Office
of the Mercury Theatre. 'Phone : Park 5700.

THE FAVIL PRESS LTD (T.U.)

ARMY EDUCATION CENTRE
FOLKESTONE.
E.N.SA. ENTERTAINMENTS FOR H. M. FORCES.

THE BOYD NEEL ORCHESTRA
(Conductor : BOYD NEEL)

with

MARK RAPHAEL (Tenor)

at the

FOLKESTONE TOWN HALL.

SUNDAY, 22nd. APRIL, at 2.30 p.m.

Branbenburg Concerto No. 3 in G	Bach.
SONGS.	
Amarilli	Caccini
Gia il Sole Dal Gange	A. Scarlatti
L'Amour de Moi	15th Century French
Mignonne alons Voir si la Rosee	14th Century French
Serenade for Strings	Elgar

INTERVAL

Capriol Suite	Peter Warlock
Shepherd Girl's Sunday	Ole Bull
SONGS	
Weep you no More	
It was a Lover	Quilter
Take O Take	
Blow Blow thou Winter Wind	
Eine Kleine Nachtmusik	Mozart

Dedicated to Miss Dinah Jones

THE LAMB

William Blake

Mark Raphael

Dedicated to my granddaughters Alexandra and Nadia

THE FLY

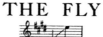

WILLIAM BLAKE

MARK RAPHAEL

Lit-tle Fly, Thy sum-mer's play My thought-less hand has brushed a-way. Am not I a fly like thee? Or art not thou A man like me? For I dance, and drink, and sing, Till some blind

1030

ROBERTON

WEEP NO MORE

Poem by
JOHN FLETCHER (1579-1625)

Music by
MARK RAPHAEL

1029

ROBERTON

ROW GENTLY HERE

Words by
THOMAS MOORE (1779-1852)

Music by
MARK RAPHAEL

Duration: 2½ mins.

1528

ROBERTON

ADON OLAM

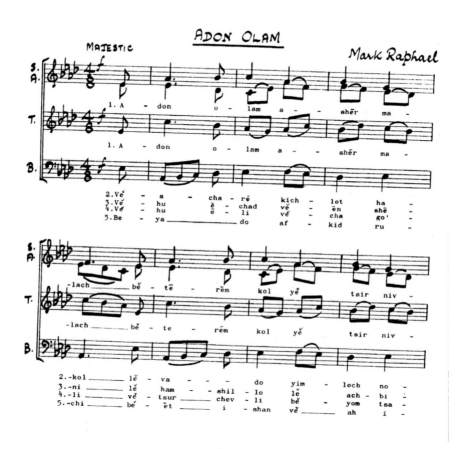

HASHIVENU

MARK RAPHAEL

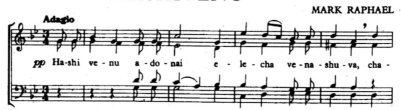

HASHIVENU

MARK RAPHAEL

Kadosh, Lechu, etc.

167

MAH TOVU (3)

MARK RAPHAEL

Mah tovu.

Gillian Thornhill is a retired teacher of languages, living in North Yorkshire, England. This is her second book, but her first biography. Apart from writing, her interests include reading, travel, music and theatre, walking in the Yorkshire countryside and interacting with friends.

Lightning Source UK Ltd.
Milton Keynes UK
UKOW040839081112

201842UK00003B/2/P